Italy
Beer Country

The Story of Italian Craft Beer

Bryan Jansing & Paul Vismara

First published by Dog Ear Publishing
4010 W. 86th Street, Ste H
Indianapolis, IN 46268
www.dogearpublishing.net

ISBN: 978-1-4575-2655-8

This book is printed on acid-free paper.

Printed in the United States of America.

All artwork and cover design by Paul Vismara.
Del Ducato art after Fortunato Depero.
All photos by Paul Vismara and Bryan Jansing, except where noted.

Table of Contents

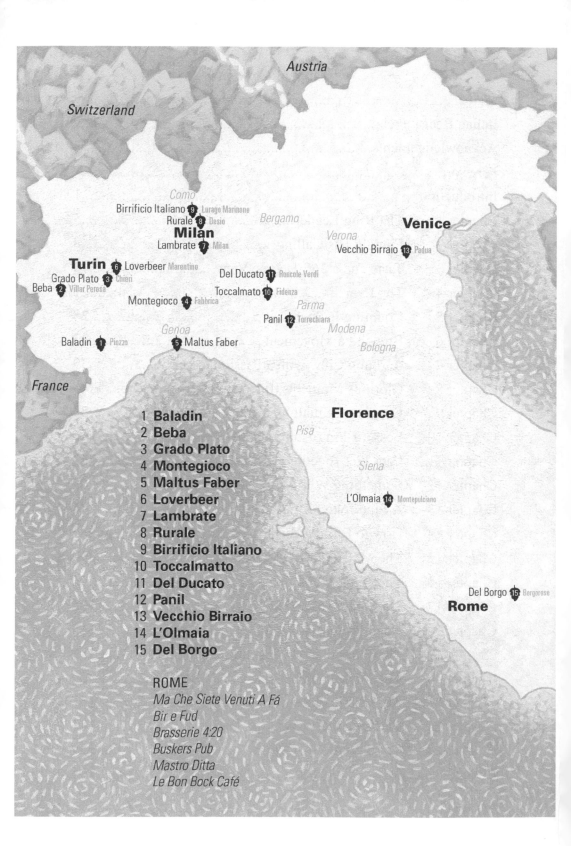

Austria

Switzerland

Como

Birrificio Italiano **9** Lurago Marinone

Bergamo

Rurale **8** Desio

Milan

Verona

Venice

Lambrate **7** Milan

Vecchio Birraio **13** Padua

Turin 6 Loverbeer Marentino

Del Ducato **11** Roncole Verdi

Grado Plato **3** Chieri

Toccalmato **10** Fidenza

Beba **2** Villar Perosa

Montegioco **4** Fabbrica

Parma

Panil **12** Torrechiara

Modena

Genoa

Bologna

Baladin **1** Piozzo

5 Maltus Faber

France

Florence

Pisa

1 **Baladin**

2 **Beba**

3 **Grado Plato**

Siena

4 **Montegioco**

5 **Maltus Faber**

6 **Loverbeer**

L'Olmaia **14** Montepulciano

7 **Lambrate**

8 **Rurale**

9 **Birrificio Italiano**

10 **Toccalmatto**

11 **Del Ducato**

12 **Panil**

Del Borgo **15** Borgorose

13 **Vecchio Birraio**

Rome

14 **L'Olmaia**

15 **Del Borgo**

ROME

Ma Che Siete Venuti A Fá

Bir e Fud

Brasserie 4:20

Buskers Pub

Mastro Ditta

Le Bon Bock Café

Acknowledgments

We could not have done this project without the help of friends, family, Kickstarter backers, and kind strangers. We would like to especially thank all the Falling Rock crew who worked for us while we traveled, our boss, Chris Black, who guided this project in the right direction from the very start, Steve Black, though he'd appreciate it more if we just said, he's a jerk. We also want to thank Alan Black for the crucial push we needed. Thanks also to the lovely, witty Fulvia Jansing who provided us with hospitality, comfort and some of the best food one could find in Italy. Thank you Eric Wallace for giving us confidence and direction. His insights at the beginning of this project provided crucial guidance which set us on the correct path. An enormous thank you to Arthur Fleisher III, Laura Keenan, Chris Norris, Kevin Reid, David Sigley, Gloria Forbes, Sam Winiser, Ed & Judy Jones, Paul Largier, Kyle (& Alex) Caldwell, Jeremy & Allison Teiber, Jeff Forbes, Leslie & Karl Fenner, David Dinges, Mike & Christy Begien, Lynn & John Tavery, Paula Dirkes, Melissa Mincic, Ernie Joynt, the Kay family, Devin Kimble, Mike & Theresa Thompson, Mark Seaman, John & Joan Vismara and Mike & Alice Israel. Anna Managó, our taxi driver in Rome, Alessandro, *Grazie, Ale*. A special thanks to our editors, Dave Krause and Alita Labak who helped steer this project with their valuable editing. Thank you Charlie Papazian, Harvey Benedict and the staff at the Vine Street Pub. And of course, to C.J. and Avery Jansing and Durinda Perkins for letting us play.

Author's Note

Throughout the book we refer to barrels and hectoliters. These are standard measurements in the beer world. One barrel of beer equals 31 US gallons. One hectoliter equals 38.7 US gallons. To convert hectoliters to barrels multiply by .8. To convert barrels to hectoliters multiply by 1.25.

We did not set out to write a comprehensive book about Italian beer styles, nor to critique the beer. *Italy: Beer Country* is a history and a guide to discovering these amazing people and their finely crafted beers. Since there are new breweries opening every week in Italy, we also did not intend to write a book that would include all the breweries in Italy.

We hope you find yourself in Italy visiting them. But be prepared to have a little patience in finding these locations. Nearly all of the breweries in Italy are very small. Many don't have any visible signage. You may have to ask for help. Sometimes online maps aren't accurate.

We went to Birrificio Del Ducato and the map led us to a house in the country. A man was out tending his garden and approached as we sat staring at what looked like a home, not a brewery. He said, "I get it all the time. They are over in Roncole Verdi." So we figured out where Roncole Verdi was and went searching. It's a tiny town, so it wasn't hard to cover the area, but we still couldn't find it. Eventually, we stopped and talked to some policemen who told us, "We think it's over there at the end of the street." We drove down to the end of the street, but the building didn't really look like a brewery and, of course, there was no sign. We stopped in the parking lot and studied the map once more. Just before leaving we saw a familiar logo on some boxes in the window; Del Ducato.

Because they are so small, many of these breweries don't have tasting rooms and aren't set up to sell beer to go. Be patient, ask politely and most all of them will do whatever they can to help.

We were fortunate to run into people like Luca Giaccone who generously gave of his time. This happened again and again. Agostino Arioli picked us up from the airport having never met us before. Teo Musso, who's always busy, spent an entire day guiding us around his various properties. The beer judge, Anna Managó, spoke with us for well over an hour giving us insights and background on the overall beer scene. The list goes on and on. We have made many great friends in the Italian beer community and can't wait to see them again and expand that circle.

As a great beer scene should, Italy's is growing with each passing week. As time passes, it will become easier and easier to find good, if not great, beer whether you're traveling in Italy or searching your local beer shop.

Please contact the authors here: birraitaliana2014@gmail.com. We will be happy to speak with you, answer questions, and hear about your Italian craft beer adventures.

Foreword

I first met Bryan and Paul about a year ago when they called me and asked for an appointment to come up to Left Hand and talk about the Italian craft beer scene. Why did they ask me? I spent seven years in the Air Force in Italy in the 1980's and 1990's and my wife Cinzia is from there. One time when I was back visiting Cinzia's family, I went to meet a friend of mine who had retired from the Air Force and was operating a restaurant in Aviano, in the Friuli region of northeastern Italy. We talked about the craft beer scene in the US and I spoke of perhaps sending some beer to Europe, since I was traveling there fairly regularly anyway. He suggested I consider going to a trade show called Pianeta Birra (Planet Beer) to meet some of the people in the beer business and get a feel for the Italian beer market.

I made three trips to Pianeta Birra in the early 2000's and met a number of wholesalers and brewers. Many of the brewers, publicans, homebrewers and beer fanatics described in this book were there, excited about their nascent beer scene and eager to fill me in on what was happening throughout Italy. They shared a lot of beer and told me about their struggles. The Italian craft beer business was quite small and felt very much like the American craft brewing scene did in the early 1990's. We had a lot in common.

The beer scene in Italy shares a few characteristics with the United States, the biggest one being an underdeveloped beer culture. It is true that beer is seen there as an accompaniment to pizza. Wine holds the high ground when it comes to pairing a drink with dinner. This is Italy, after all. Beer culture there is somewhat vestigial, a remnant of German and Slavic influences through centuries of invasions, wars, trading and tourism. American beer culture had been strong, but was virtually wiped out after Prohibition, reduced primarily to light lagers almost indistinguishable from each other. The result was a vocabulary unable to fully describe the breadth of the beer world, the plethora of styles, flavors, and aromas, both in Italian and in English.

We've been educating American beer drinkers (and ourselves as brewers) for decades, so here we have pretty much resolved that language problem. Pale ales and IPAs, porters, stouts, bitters, Lambics and imperial everythings are part of our common vernacular today. Our Italian brethren still struggle against the chains of "chiara (clear or light), rossa (red), scura (dark), doppio malto (double malt or strong)". They often have to adopt English and French or Flemish words to accurately describe their work. They are faced with an educational effort that will last decades to build an awareness of the wide world of beer that we are so fortunate to enjoy in the US today.

To their credit, they have the passion and creativity to brew beers of magnificent complexity and flavor. Italy's lack of a beer culture presents a clean slate upon which the Italian brewer/artist can express himself. Italy has an unbelievably diverse array of culinary traditions. Autochthonous foods and strong regional differences make the country a test brew system for exploring creativity and terroir in beer making like few other places I know. I see strong parallels to the American beer scene, where we first imitated, then improved, then hybridized and ultimately went completely off the map and created many new styles. The Italian beer scene is every bit as creative as ours—it's just a bit less visible than our scene here in the US. They have higher hurdles to overcome.

I intend to use this book, *Italy: Beer Country*, as a guide to future trips back to Italy to visit some wonderful breweries and pubs. I hope it inspires the reader to get over to Italy and explore its incredible, blossoming beer scene and to urge these pioneers to greater things!

Eric Wallace
President
Left Hand Brewing Company
December, 2013

This book is dedicated to my father, Thomas J. Jansing.
Thanks for the passion, pops.

Introduction

My taste for beer stems from my father. Born in Cincinnati, he was a big fan of German-style lagers and of quality beer in general. He wasn't much of a drinker, but he enjoyed a good beer and was never shy to offer me some. I loved it. When I turned fourteen years old, we moved to Vicenza in northern Italy.

Being near the Austrian border, it was commonplace to find various styles of German and Austrian lagers. I was old enough in Italy to drink and took to discovering these beers with a passion. I wouldn't say I was a beer nerd, necessarily, but more of a beer drinker with a thirst for very good beer.

When I moved to Denver, I started working at one of the most important American tap houses, the Falling Rock Tap House.

"Our friendship began in 1998," recalls Paul Vismara, Illustrator, "ever since I started going to the Falling Rock Tap House for their unrivaled selection of craft beer. I moved from Chicago to Denver and knew of Falling Rock. The day the moving truck left, I walked the six blocks to check it out. I immediately liked the casual, sarcastic vibe of the staff, and you couldn't find a better beer selection in the state. Falling Rock became my place of choice, and I eventually got to know most everyone who worked there, including Bryan.

"I attended art school in Pasadena, California, in the late 1980s. This was a time when American craft beer was slowly getting underway, and California had two of the most vibrant and important players, Anchor and Sierra Nevada. Whenever I had the chance, the first thing I'd do when entering a bar was look for the oval Anchor labels or the green Sierra Nevada Pale Ale label. Any beer fan from that era remembers the constant search."

While I was in Rome visiting my parents in 2012, a friend suggested I check out Trastevere: "That's where you'll find beer."

I took my friend's advice and stepped into a pizzeria called Bir e Fud with several Italian craft beers on tap. Both my wife and I were surprised. What had happened here? This was incredible. When had this all happened? We had no idea.

Back in Denver, near the end of that summer, I was reflecting on my experience in Rome to Paul, who is truly a beer nerd. It was just a conversation, nothing more than a reflection while having a beer at the Falling Rock. Paul speaks Italian, has traveled there often, and loves Rome almost as much as I do.

"This project began with a foggy-brained phone call in the summer of 2012," Paul says. "I had just moved, in the midst of a very busy period, and with the stress wasn't sleeping well. The alarm went off, and I stumbled down the stairs with thoughts swirling through my still-asleep brain. I poured a cup of yesterday's coffee, nuked it, and picked up the phone to call Bryan. 'Hey, we should write a book about Italian craft beer.'

"'Hell, yeah,' Bryan replied. 'That's a *great* idea!'

"We had been looking for a project to work on together almost from the time we first met nearly fifteen years ago. Bryan has been a writer for fifteen years, and I have been a freelance illustrator for nearly twenty-five. It was always in the back of our minds, but nothing had come along that we were both excited about. This was it. This was our project. We could bring all our passions together: writing, illustration, and beer in one book.

"The first person we approached was our boss, Chris Black, owner of the Falling Rock, who has a wealth of beer knowledge. He didn't know much about Italian beer, but he did know someone who might, Eric Wallace."

Eric is the founder of Left Hand Brewing, not far from Denver in Longmont, Colorado. He has lived in Europe, is married to an Italian, and speaks the language fluently. He was very familiar with the movement and knew many brewers, writers, critics, and publicans. We handed him a list of Italian breweries and asked him to point out the most important ones.

Paul and I knew we were onto something. We had no idea how we were going to tackle this, but we knew we had to. During one of our late-night meetings, we finally decided to simply call some of these brewers and see if they would be available to talk to us if we flew out there. We called Agostino Arioli first.

Agostino was a stranger to us, but he readily made himself available and even offered to pick us up when we arrived in Milan. Agostino was gracious and set us on the right course. As we went through Eric Wallace's checklist and began to collect interviews for this story, we were continually humbled. All the people we met gave us their time generously and encouraged us.

To any beer lover reading this, we hope you find the chance to visit our new friends in Italy. They will treat you with all the charm and love Italians are famous for. They are imaginative, creative, and extraordinary craftsmen—but everything you need to know about them, you'll discover in their beer.

In Bocca Al Luppolo,

Bryan and Paul

Paul Vismara (left) and Bryan Jansing (right).
Photo by Fabio Mozzone

Chapter 1
The Ring Leader

In the wee hours of a foggy night in 1996, a truck driven by Monsieur Jean-Luis Dits meanders through the tight, winding streets of the Langhe (pronounced Lah-n-gay), a dialect word for the hilly, rural region in the southern part of Piedmont best known for its Barolo and Barbera wines. The tiny truck's load may as well be from outer space: a huge, wood-paneled, pan-shaped vat only inches from toppling many of the first-story balconies along its way.

Dits, the Belgian brewer and owner of Brasserie Vapeur in Pipaix, Belgium, has been to the Langhe before, but with such a large payload, it's nearly impossible to use the same tight roads he took in his car. Too tired to be scared, Dits presses through—all he can think about is finding Baladin and getting to sleep.

Then, in the deep Piedmont fog, a single vehicle overtakes him and pulls over in front of the truck.

What is this foolish man doing? Dits thinks.

"The man jumped out of his car and asked me, 'Baladin?'" Dits recalls.

By chance, the lunatic is Mauro, an employee and friend of the proprietor of the new beer vat that has been wandering the small byways of the Langhe for several hours in the blinding fog.

"We were saved," Dits exclaims.

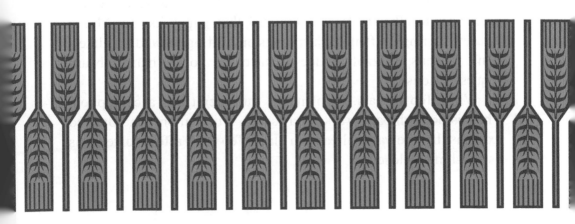

With Mauro as a guide, the vat, Dits, and history are in place. Italy is on its way to becoming a beer country.

As Teo Musso, owner of the vat and Baladin, often does, he acts before thinking. After buying the vat, Teo returned home to Piozzo to prepare a space for his new vessel—except, he had no space. His landlady has consistently refused his requests to rent her garage next to the pub. Away on her six-month sabbatical in San Remo, she can't say no, so Teo becomes a squatter. He empties her garage and prepares it for the new vat already on its way.

When his landlady returns and finds her belongings replaced with some foreign vessel bubbling with beer, she flips. After many quarrels and threats from his landlady to call the police, Teo calms her by offering to rent another garage for her belongings.

With the vat situated, Teo closes his ten-year-old beer bar, Le Baladin. Gone are all 200 labels and the many patrons he's coddled over the years, but Teo knows he's onto something. He doesn't fret. Le Baladin undergoes some renovations, transforming into something never heard of before in Italy—an artisanal brewpub. He has to add a tap system to the once bottle-only beer bar. There will be no beer sold at Le Baladin except Baladin beer.

Dits leaves Christian Vanhaverbeke, his assistant brewer at Brasserie Vapeur, to help Teo and returns home, perhaps unaware that he's just detonated a movement. Not more than a month in, the vat catches fire as Teo attempts a couple of recipes.

With disaster avoided and the vat repaired, Teo takes the next step: to get approval and licensing for his new contraption and philosophy. At the Guardia di Finanza, Italy's bureaucratic department of excise, licensing, revenue, and anything to do with business, Signore Cozzolino has no idea that his world is about to be turned upside down. When he first sees the tall, thin, gypsy-like Teo Musso wearing earrings, a flannel shirt, rings on his fingers, and hair like a punk rocker's, Cozzolino doesn't take the young man's absurd request seriously.

When Teo reveals his plan, the bureaucrat has a conniption. There is no such paperwork for a "small, artisanal brewer." But Teo explains that the vat is already in place. Teo can't afford to keep his establishment closed.

After much arguing, Cozzolino resigns himself to the idea that if he just gets this weird man out of his office on a long journey of paperwork and permits, the man won't return. He hands Teo a list of complicated files and forms to complete, and letters to write.

Twenty or so days later, Teo returns with a briefcase full of hand-written crumpled forms and requests. It's only then that Cozzolino realizes the strange young man is dead serious. The bureaucrat relents. When he brings Teo's paperwork to his bosses in Turin, they laugh at him. Every week, Teo calls Cozzolino, who has to explain to the impatient Teo that the approval is going to take some time. Cozzolino works through the endless bureaucratic obstacles for three months to create documents for something that has never existed before, but Teo's hard-fought requests are finally approved.

Teo has been working at a feverish pitch for a solid two months reinventing Le Baladin, which has been closed since the vat's arrival. The risk of reopening to find no patrons is high. Teo's first batches of beer are a light ale and an amber he simply names Blond and Amber. While he is still refining his techniques, the two beers aren't necessarily appreciated by his patrons, who drink Teo's beer with indifference and suspicion. There are prejudices as well. The idea that you can brew a beer locally just doesn't occur to the people of Piozzo.

"Very high-end wines are made in the Langhe. It was very difficult to begin producing beer here. It didn't exist. There wasn't anything," Teo says.

These were difficult times for Le Baladin and Teo Musso.

Chapter 2
Finding His Calling

Matterino "Teo" Musso's journey to brewer begins while he is visiting his uncle Celso, the pastry chef of Hotel Paris in Monte Carlo. As a teen, Teo spends his summers visiting his uncle. Far from the little village in the ocean of vineyards and rolling green hills is a world completely different than the land of farmers that is his home. Monte Carlo is a city of millionaires, with exotic foods and eclectic tastes.

When Teo first tries beer as a young man, he is completely disgusted by the industrial beers available, such as Peroni and Moretti. He takes great pleasure in aggravating his father, though, by drinking beer instead of wine at the table. Wine has been on the Italian table for more than a millennium, but beer is regarded as a thirst-quencher for the laborers, so putting beer on the table is like putting your feet on the table. Beer, at best, is something to drink with pizza, like Coke and a hotdog. While on vacation in Monte Carlo, Teo has the chance to try what will change not just his taste but, essentially, Italy's. With one sip of the Chimay Blue, the iconic, richly flavored Trappist beer, the world of Italian beer marks a shift. Teo is struck by the strong character, the fragrance, the lingering malt with notes of figs and dates.

This newly discovered flavor for great beer sets Teo off on a long journey to learn more. He spends years trying and tasting and expanding his knowledge. At home, beer continues to be a means for a rebellious teenager to irk his wine-drinking father.

Overlooking the single steeple and bell tower is Piozzo's small piazza, no bigger than a baseball field. Beyond the two tiny roads that lead into and out of the square is a wave of green hills that roll to the horizon on all sides touching the hazy Piedmont sky. Teo's father, like many farmers in this area, made his own wines to drink at home with meals. It's not that Teo doesn't like wine, but beer...something in the taste of beer captivates the young Teo.

"I was born the son of a farmer in wine country. My mom and dad are eighty-nine and eighty-five years old with sixty-seven years of marriage," Teo says. "They are country folk. They're good people. We put the cantina in the chicken coop where they were born. My dad made simple house wine. My parents are very simple, they never had a honeymoon; they've never even left Piozzo."

One summer with his uncle in Monte Carlo, Teo meets the beautiful ballet dancer Michele and the couple falls in love. Teo, who doesn't drive or own a moped like many Italian teens, takes buses and trains to reach Monte Carlo on the weekends. On many of his return trips, the buses never show and he has to walk kilometers, over hills, to reach home. During the week, because he doesn't drive, he's often late to work as a blacksmith for his older brother.

The quirks of the young Teo are not strange to his family, however. The youngest of four, Teo is the baby of the Musso family. No one really had time to worry over little Teo; everyone was busy working. His oldest brother is nearly twenty years older.

"I was born March 5, 1964, by accident," Teo explains.

As a teen, the rebellious Teo wears makeup and combs his hair in the punk and new-wave styles. "I was a disaster at school. I chose for my high school the one with the most girls. My parents were embarrassed." No one scolds him. He is their eccentric Teo.

Perhaps this is what captivates the young Michele, a distant cousin of Teo's. By 1986, Teo, now twenty-two years old, and Michele, also young at twenty-one, are ready to take the next step in their relationship. Monte Carlo is far too expensive for a young ballerina and smith to find a means to survive, so they decide they will live in Piozzo.

"I love where I'm from, this countryside," he says.

Teo's father gives each of his sons ten million lira, or about $8,000, to use in any way the sons wish when they leave home. Teo decides he will use his allotment to open a bar where he grew up, in Piozzo—but not just any bar. This bar will have a list of exceptional beer from Belgium, Germany, and England. And there will be no soccer or sports of any kind. In fact, on Cup Wednesdays, the day when important soccer games are played, Teo will bring in live music. His friends think he's out of his mind. Who will show up on what is the equivalent of Super Bowl Sundays to hear local live bands and drink exotic beers when there are pivotal soccer matches to watch?

The concept for Le Baladin, and everything Baladin, takes its inspiration from a French traveling circus of acrobats, jugglers, singers, dancers, and performers owned by Francois "Bidon" Rauline. The French meaning of "baladin" is buffoon or jester. Each year, Rauline's French circus, Bidon, treks through the Langhe by horse with exotically painted and decorated carriages. In Italy, these circuses are known as street theaters and are much like the American Vaudeville shows in their heyday.

"Before I opened Le Baladin in 1986," Teo says, "I traveled with the show. When I opened the bar, the people from the French circus Bidon helped me do the construction. The following year, they did the show in Piozzo with chickens walking a tightrope and performances like that. It's a circus from another time."

Walking into the pub Le Baladin is like stepping into a circus tent. Performing elephants are painted alongside juggling clowns next to brightly colored striped walls that take you in and lead you to the main room, where a circus tent in miniature looms overhead. An image of a knife thrower's assistant is painted on a wall, with the freshly thrown knives around her acting as coat hangers, while images of trapeze artists swing overhead and posters of circus shows of the past are pasted all over the faux tent walls. "Gusto Baladin is a separate department that does all the artwork with two cinematographers and two painters that work for me," Teo explains. "They do everything—the balconies, the taps, the sinks, the columns. We make the steel to make the columns. Every aspect is made by us." It's truly an experience.

As Teo puts it, "With beer and music, miracles can happen." To this day, Wednesday is live music night at Le Baladin.

After acquiring an importer's license, Teo builds a list of beer from abroad that reaches more than 200. In 1986, no other such place exists in Italy. Perhaps a few bars in the north feature German beer, even some Belgian, but none list 200 beers, and certainly no pubs as eccentric and awe-inspiring as Le Baladin. Even today, Le Baladin stands out as one of the most interesting, exotic, and innovative bars in the world. To have entered this remarkable space in the mid-1980s, to drink beer, in, of all places, the Langhe, would have

Le Baladin.

been more than just extraordinary. It simply would have been out of this world.

But this is, after all, Teo Musso's trait and talent: to bring his imagination to fruition in a physical world and allow you to become enthralled with his inner mind by way of a physical space through drink, food, and sound.

Teo's success allows him in 1994 to open a location in Strasbourg, France, where the servers glide by on roller skates. Unbeknownst to him, his partner running the bar in Strasbourg develops a heavy drinking habit. By the time Teo realizes the dire straits, the Strasbourg business flops. He is heartbroken. This is his first failure, and though it was out of his hands, it hurts.

While in Strasbourg shutting down the defunct bar, Teo discovers his first brewery and brewpub. He's blown away by the concept, and an idea ferments in his mind.

At Le Baladin, Michele and Teo's relationship sours. After nearly a decade, they break up. As Teo puts it, they were young when they married and simply grew apart. Teo takes his anguish to Belgium, driven by the curiosity of creating a brewpub in Italy.

"In 1995 I took a course and began to learn about beer production. I wasn't interested in making beer; I was interested in *how* it was made. Over time, my interest in making beer began to grow."

He knows he's onto something because nobody else in Italy is doing such a thing. As far as he knows, an artisanal brewpub has never existed in his country. While traveling through Belgium in search of beers to add to his list at Le Baladin, Teo talks to brewers to amass more knowledge about the art of brewing. It's during this time when he meets an Algerian woman named Nora.

While visiting Nora's parents in Valenciennes on the border of France and Belgium, Teo and Nora travel to the small Belgian town of Pipaix and by chance find themselves at Brasserie Vapeur—owned by Jean-Luis Dits. For Teo, meeting Dits "changed my life, just as the Chimay Blue did."

"I liked Teo immediately. But at first I thought he was a bit crazy," Dits says. "I was building a small brewing system for a brewery in Athens when Teo and Nora arrived. Teo saw the different vats and asked to know what it was for. I told him. He then asked, 'Could you build one for me? Do you think I'm able to brew?' I said, 'Well, you don't seem too stupid. You should be able to.'"

"Jean-Luis Dits was one of my teachers. I had two teachers: Dits, who was creative, and Christian Vanhaverbeke, who was technical. It gave me a good balance. They were complete opposites. With Christian, I began by replicating the recipe for Chimay. In reality, we made those kinds of beers because we needed to lean on those great beers for a good start. Mainly, I was depending on the masters to teach me the technical side of things. But Dits gave me a completely different vision."

"When you're inspired to make a beer and you drink it and it's terrible," Jean-Luis Dits tells Teo one day, "don't worry about it. There will come a day when it finds its balance and it's good for your palate."

"I thought the guy was crazy," Teo says.

"Let's say you're making a beer," Dits says, "and it gets infected. Don't worry about it. Give it two years and the beer will fix itself."

"It opened doors for me," Teo says. "I could think well beyond where I was. For recipes and research, I could think in terms of years, too."

Chapter 3
Taste and a 360-Degree View

From the moment Le Baladin reopens as a brewpub, Teo's hours are long. He works the bar through midnight, then brews into the early hours of the morning. At nine a.m., he goes to bed, then sleeps until one p.m., only to return to tend bar and repeat the cycle. He also spends time reinventing his kitchen to better match the beer he's brewing.

Within the first year of becoming a brewery, Le Baladin comes to life. Teo moves past his initial brews of a light ale and amber to create three new styles: a blanche, a bruin, and an abbey. People are talking, and stories are being written about this strange concept of Italian artisanal beer, so much so that a beer critic hearing of this crazy idea decides to visit.

When Lorenzo Dabove, the great beer aficionado from Genoa, best known by his pseudonym, Kuaska, first tries Teo's beer, he describes the first two as rather unpleasant, but, as he puts it, his professionalism as a beer critic, writer, and taster forces him to try all three. The last one, the abbey…now that's something. It's nothing spectacular, but the abbey served in the proper glass is enough to convince Kuaska that things at Baladin are serious. He's never tasted an Italian beer in this style and of this caliber. It still needs work, but it is a true beer. He has three glasses of the abbey before asking to meet the brewer. Teo is ecstatic. Even though he's a bit heartbroken by the critiques of the first two beers, Teo's never met an Italian beer critic.

With suggestions from Kuaska, Teo's beer develops. Teo leaps from his abbey toward something original and completely unique in 1997 with his Super.

For Teo, the Super is fundamentally the beginning of everything that Baladin beer is today. To start, the Super originates from an old Belgian abbey beer recipe from 800 CE. With aromas of flowers, apricot, and banana and hints of almond, the Super is a sophisticated leap from Teo's original brews created less than a year before.

He finds his stride and picks up the pace. As soon as his son, Isaac, is born on August 25, 1997, Teo leaves the hospital for the brewery and spends the entire night, with a joyful heart, setting a precedent that will become his trait: brewing with his emotions to make works of art.

Teo creates his next beer, Isaac.

"My ideas are always from an emotion. I try to translate those emotions from my head. For me, beer is a language of communication, a way of speaking. It's not that different from an artist expressing himself, but if you're good, you're amplifying these living tastes. Even when I send beer far away, I need the emotions to come through. This 360-degree view is what I feel: the beer, the art, the music, everything."

Teo Musso in his barrel room.

The Isaac is a blanche turned Mediterranean by substituting the regular orange peels and coriander with Mediterranean oranges and grains from Italy.

"When we started," says Baladin's head brewer, Paolo "Palli" Fontana, "we could make whatever we wanted. Isaac is a blanche, but it is our interpretation of a blanche. We try to do this in an Italian way."

That winter, Teo creates the Noël, a full-bodied Christmas beer in the Belgian style. Teo likes it so much, he decides to keep the Noël year-round but changes the Christmas name, Noël to Lëon, which is Noël spelled backward. Each year, the Lëon is released again as Noël, a holiday beer, but always with a different twist, such as adding vanilla for a special holiday treat.

Moreover, Teo decides to do something that will launch not just Le Baladin but Italian beer altogether into the bigger picture. Teo has been weighing the idea of bottling his beer. This is an idea that goes further than just allowing the consumer to carry his beer out of the brewpub; it is an idea with a grander marketing strategy, one that reveals Teo Musso's far-reaching vision.

"The first bottle I made was Super, and I made it with this particular cap. It is similar to ones used for champagne, but this one is a miniature version. The flange isn't as long. This is the first bottle in this style that doesn't have the cage. By making this type of cap versus the cage style used on champagne bottles, an 800-cage production turns into 3,000 with this cap. It will hold up to five bars of pressure, or about sixty pounds of atmospheric pressure. Champagne is at seven bars. I also manufactured the cap so if the beer gets too hot, it will pop off."

Teo spends hours placing his bottles into an oven to perfect his caps so they pop at just the right temperature, the temperature at which the beer will be damaged if left in the sun or in a hot car. Always a micromanager, Teo finds a means to remain omnipresent with his products.

After months of work, Teo settles on a shapely bottle of 75 centiliters with very elegant labels that no one would have connected with beer. The genius behind the idea is to elevate artisanal beer onto the table alongside wine at restaurants that serve sophisticated foods. In 1997, this isn't a mere marketing move; it's a coup, a farfetched leap into no-man's land. No one ever has attempted such a thing before, especially in Italy.

"We always want our beer to pair well with food," Palli says. "The idea is that our beer must always be attractive for restaurants. We think of our beer as being on a table at a restaurant. Even if we make an IPA, we think of that beer on the table and make a softer IPA."

For Italians, wine and food are a sacred combination, but Teo understands that the Italian palate will embrace the depth of flavors in beer and find that it can pair well with food.

"Taste is my main point. It's a 360-degree view. All of the bottles, the presentation, it all matters, but it's all about the taste. Without taste, there's nothing else. The Italian market is much, much harder to crack because we are pickier about what we eat and drink."

The challenge is to overcome the cultural concept that beer is a hotdog, low class.

"Teo wanted a bottle that could sit next to a wine bottle and not seem out of place," Fabio Mozzone, Director of Marketing, says. "Before, restaurants weren't open to this concept. We took a different approach with the labels as well, making the name of the beer more prominent than the name of the brewery. People thought he was crazy to make the brewery name so small on the labels, but it worked. People began asking for the beer by its name. We want customers to learn the names of the beers so they will associate the taste with the name of the product. It was expensive, but it was great marketing. He doesn't use a typical approach. It's very natural for him."

Teo's next step is to place the bottles: "I found 500 restaurants that I believed cared about taste and quality. I brought them three beers each." He packs the three bottles into a case and personally drives them to 500 well-chosen, high-end restaurants all over Italy. "The reason I went to the very best restaurants was to bring beer up to that high level. It was a small amount, but still, it was all over. Without that, beer wouldn't have gone anywhere in Italy."

"Teo started by bottling the beer and going directly to the wine sellers from 1997 to 2000," says Franco "Cico" Fallarini, sales manager at Selezione Baladin, Teo's distribution company. Cico previously worked in a large commercial clothing company and a large soft drink company.

Cico is Teo's first waiter from the first day Le Baladin opened twenty-seven years ago. "On his first day, he spilled a container all over some customers." Teo says.

"I've known Teo for thirty-four years, since we were children," Cico says. "He's always been charismatic. Teo would walk into a restaurant looking like a gypsy, but they bought his beer. They started to recognize Teo and they started to try the beer."

The impression becomes disillusion when Teo learns that the main drinkers of his beer aren't the patrons of the restaurants, but the staff. The chefs and servers love Teo's beer, but they don't have the courage to place the bottles on the tables and risk offending their patrons.

"They didn't sell them to their clients, but they kept buying our beer," Cico says. "It really began to happen in 2000 when a sommelier mentioned they were drinking our beer to a representative of high-end Barolo wines in Bologna. The sommelier said to the rep, 'I drank a beer from Teo Musso. Do you want to try it? Only my staff drinks it.' The rep tried it and really liked it and said, 'I can sell this beer in Bologna.' It grew by word of mouth. Then a small wine distributor in Tuscany began to sell our beer in the wine world. We took what Teo had started and expanded it."

"I went to an association that sold the best wines in Italy," Teo says. "And they got it. They tried my beer and understood right away. They thought restaurants would fall in love with this over time. So they placed a bet on it."

From this point, Baladin beer is distributed to the finest restaurants in Italy by a greatly respected distributor of fine wines and, now, fine beer. With Teo's endless and energetic travels to promote, teach, and encourage locals to drink Italian-made artisanal beer, things begin to develop. It is an enormous leap for the infant craft-beer movement, but one that will continue to build strength and momentum by way of Slow Foods.

When McDonald's opens in Rome in 1986, it sparks a protest that reverberates through Italian culture. Carlo Petrini, a food and wine writer born in Bra in the Langhe, is so indignant about the mass-processed fast-food garbage being foisted upon Italy's long-held traditions that he sets off a revolution—Slow Food, the antithesis of fast food: seasonal, local, and made by hand. The movement begun by Petrini is closely felt by Teo. The connection between Slow Food and artisanal beer makes sense from the start. Both movements share the goal of local production for freshness, taste, and better health. The forged alliance grows hand in hand.

In 1996, Teo visits the first Slow Food festival, known in Italy as the Salone Del Gusto. He carries two beers, literally a beer in each hand, to be tasted. To show up at a festival with only two beers in hand seems like a joke at the time, but it soon becomes a synergy that will continue to develop and promote Italian artisanal beer. Through the Salone Del Gusto in 1998, the Italian artisanal beer gets a boost when the world-famous beer writer Michael Jackson is invited. His being at the event is an unspoken acknowledgment that Italian craft beer has merit.

At the same time, Marco Bolasco, a young writer looking to make his mark decides to write a piece about beer in the prestigious Italian food and wine magazine *Gambero-Rosso*. Marco feels he has a better chance to be heard by writing about this unknown artisanal beer. He begins by interviewing Teo Musso. This then leads to a beer tasting at a wine-tasting event. The presence of beer at such a high-profile event is a first in Italian history and an important step toward elevating Italian craft beer in the minds of the Italian public.

"To get Italians to drink different beer was the challenge," Teo says. "I wasn't going to change the Italian palate for beer. I didn't see it that way."

Teo has set the pace. His ideas of what beer can be in Italy continue to grow. In 1996, less than a year into his project, Teo sees a larger picture, one that goes beyond Piozzo. But there is another component in the works.

On that fateful day when Kuaska comes by to check out Teo's brewpub in Piozzo, he drops a bombshell just before leaving.

"You know," Kuaska says, "there's another man who's opened a brewpub in a little town near Como." He digs through his bag and finds a coaster he has been carrying with him. He hands the coaster to Teo. It reads, Birrificio Italiano.

Chapter 4
The Bear

"At the beginning there were two different approaches—Teo and me. Teo was brewing beer in wine country for people who didn't like beer. And so the food was more important, that's why he never used a lot of hops. Nowadays he uses some, but at the beginning he was doing a blanche, with low hops, a malty beer with no hops, a saison with no hops, and so on. He was aiming for the wine market. He's a great marketer and he did it very efficiently, but not for German-style drinkers. Hops were important to me. Hops are something beer lovers like—the bitterness. I was brewing beer for beer lovers, not necessarily for beer experts—session beers. I just wanted to give a new chance to beer drinkers to simply drink beer."

Agostino Arioli launches his brewery, Birrificio Italiano, in Lurago Marinone, a sleepy little town of about 2,500 people located twenty miles northwest of Milan in the province of Como, in the Lombard region. Lurago Marinone's oldest church, San Giorgio, built in 1216, is the only reminder that this was once an important town. With the city of Milan looming nearby, it would seem tiny Lurago Marinone is the most unlikely place to find the epicenter of a beer movement.

"When we found this building, I said, 'I like this place, but we are in Lurago Marinone. I never knew where Lurago Marinone was,

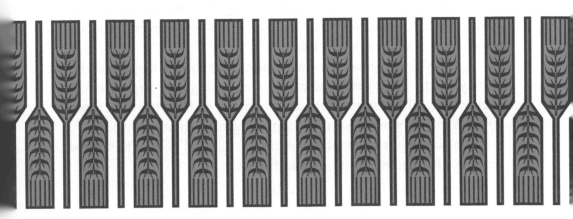

and I was living six kilometers from here.' Lurago Marinone was a bit exotic, even for me," Agostino says.

Birrificio Italiano is poised on a small hill under the shade of a large horse chestnut tree. A narrow, curvy road passes below like a brush stroke and leads in and out of the town. At the main intersection is a traffic light. A parking lot, perhaps the largest open space in Lurago Marinone, rests across the street under the gaze of the patio where the bells of San Giorgio sound the passing hours.

The sun streams in through the large windows of the brewpub, lighting the white walls adorned with a few beer-related decorations. The brass tap system is capable of pouring eight beers and has one hand-pull. In the back room, a large hall opens, with several wooden tables, with a kitchen on the left.

In 1996, the original brewing equipment takes up a space about twenty feet by twenty feet and can be seen through the large window facing the road as patrons walk in. Crossing over from the front room to the back is a glass floor panel with a mirror hanging down.

"The cellar was downstairs. A mirror allowed people to see the fermentation and maturation tanks below."

The first impression, if you're an Italian, is that there is only beer on all the tables, not a wine or pizza in sight. It smacks against what every Italian is used to seeing when there is beer. The food has a touch of the Trentino cuisine with its Slavic, Austrian, and Hungarian influences, because this is what Agostino and his brother Stefano's mother taught them. Items such as Tuscan salumis and a potato polenta are also served without the German cliché of sausage, brat, or pretzel.

"I never designed my beer thinking about food. What we did here was quite a brave choice never to pair the beer with those kinds of German foods that the town expected. Never. I wrote down on all of our promotional flyers, 'no wurst, no kraut, no French fries.' So we paired the Italian kitchen with beer. But never, never, never was my beer born thinking about food, because food follows beer. I always tell people, drink the beer without food."

The brewery, like the town, is an unlikely candidate to hold a great title, but it does. It's here, in 1996, that Agostino and Stefano begin a brewery that will define a cultural phenomenon and redefine the image of a wine country. With Italy's long and outstanding culinary history, it's amazing that beer has remained absent from its cuisine, not to mention craft beer. The last person from this area to leave an impact on beer was the Roman nobleman Pliny the Elder, who was born in Como and gave hops their Latin name, Humulus Lupulus—Italians call it Luppolo. It's in this faraway little town that Agostino writes a new chapter in Italy's culinary history.

A contrarian at heart, the Bear, as Agostino is sometimes called, is one of the most important people in the Italian craft-beer movement. A no-nonsense kind of man, Agostino's the type who can become easily annoyed by stupidity or ignorance. Slender, with short-cropped hair, a receding hairline, and a graying goatee, Agostino has soft eyes that absorb the world around him. He holds the bearing of a professor and, when humored, won't burst into laughter but give you the warm, rich smile of a person who's always contemplating. He has a knack for precision and a patience that allows time to work in his favor. In 1996, he's going to need all this character and talent to demonstrate to the always-suspicious Italian that quality artisanal beer can be brewed in this country. Agostino

Agostino Arioli.

has a long way to go to wash away the common misconception that beer is the cold, not-very-good-smelling, clear drink so strongly promoted by Moretti and Peroni. Perhaps this could have only derived from a man who refuses to allow style to define his beer or history to define what is legitimate.

"Styles are something I really love and hate," explains Agostino. "It helps me to orient, but it also sometimes feels that styles are a bottleneck for beer culture. I think you should drink a beer without knowing what style it is. I suggest at beer tastings to ignore style. Just drink your beer, have your sense experience, and just judge if it's pleasant or not. Then judge the style it's supposed to be. Even despite this, some people look for style. They don't drink the beer; they drink the style. It's stupid, because in that way, you're drinking with your mind, not with your senses."

Agostino's long trek to becoming brewer at Birrificio Italiano starts at the age of fourteen. "I was a beer drinker at a very young age. Too young, I would say."

Even though the drinking age in Italy is sixteen, in the late 1970s, there are a few places that allow Agostino and his friends to dabble in beer.

"At that time, we had some beer from the Italian brewery Birra Forst, who still brew, and make a kind of dopplebock that is quite strong, like 8 percent alcohol by volume." Forst was founded in 1857 in Merano, Italy, near the Austrian border. Today, it has an annual production of 700,000 hectoliters, or about 560,000 barrels. "But there were German and English beers on draft like Bulldog, John Martin, and Courage Bitter, my personal favorite." German weizens are just getting a footing in Italy in the early 1980s. EKU and EKU 28 are two very strong beers that Agostino and his friends discover, along with small amounts of Belgian beer, like Chimay. "We were just young kids, but we were revolutionary in our way. There was an aim to change toward something different. We chose beer, not wine."

Admittedly a lazy student in college, Agostino has time on his hands, so he takes his beer interest to the next level and decides to try home brewing. In Italy in 1985, there's no such thing as home brewing. There are no shops that sell brewing material, books, or, most important, supplies. Agostino devises a small carboy, typically a five-gallon vessel used to ferment home-brewed beer. With the difficulty of finding material in Italy, Agostino's passion presses him to take whatever measures necessary to brew beer. With no place to get malt, he makes his own and uses bread yeast to ferment the beer.

"I dumped everything because it was unbelievably awful. Preparing your own malt is too difficult. You never know if you did something wrong malting or brewing."

But he's made his first attempt, and the game is on. In 1986, Agostino's father, always attentive to his bright son's whims, locates a resource in this beer desert. "He found a man, a friend that had a connection with an existing brewery. So finally, through this man, I got in touch with a brewer that was working in the beer industry named Gianni Pasa. Gianni started to give me suggestions, tips about brewing, equipment, and he gave me some fresh yeast, some malt and hops."

Agostino's father later gives him a fermenter with the ability to control brewing temperatures.

"I started brewing lager beer because the available fresh yeast was lager yeast, not really because I was more fond of lager beer than ales, but Gianni was a German-oriented brewer, so he knew a lot about those styles. I went on brewing, more or less, the same beer for ten years or more.

"I still suggest to all home brewers who want to learn to brew to stay on one beer for one year or two years. You check your equipment for slight differences, details. It's much more important than changing your recipe every time like you're looking for a special beer, a crazy one, the *final* beer. No, you'll never find it. If you're a home brewer who just wants to have fun, it's okay to change your recipe every time, but if you want to learn brewing, stick with one, maximum two, recipes, like the great painters who start in another great painter's shop mixing colors for one or two years and that's it."

Germany in 1986 is bucking its own trend and moving away from the historical village breweries and opening some new-wave brewpubs in cities and larger towns. Gianni is the first to suggest that Agostino open a brewpub. On one of several trips to Germany to learn beer, Agostino visits a friend in Berlin who brings him to one of these new pubs, Der Vogelbräu in Karlsruhe. Agostino now understands Gianni's suggestion, and it sets him on a course to invent the Italian brewpub.

Even though Agostino realizes his direction, at twenty-one years old, he still isn't ready to take on responsibilities. Attracted by the forests and the lakes, he decides instead to take a two-month dream trip to Canada, alone. He visits friends in Toronto, then weaves his way through the Rocky Mountains to Vancouver, British Columbia. There he finds the Granville Island Brewery, which opened in 1984; one of the first brewpubs in North America.

Upon Agostino's return, perhaps with a bit of worry for his aimless son, his father proposes a deal. Friends from Tuscany have a small house for sale, but it needs a lot of renovation. "We went to visit this very old, small house. My father said to me, 'If you take care of all the renovation, I will buy the house.' I, being stupid said, yes, okay."

For the next year, Agostino renovates the small house near Pienza in southern Tuscany.

"We rebuilt the house. It was a great experience."

Italy in the 1980s still has a military draft. Service can be postponed while in school, but after his year in Tuscany, Agostino's time has run out. He begins his obligatory year-long service. Finally, with the arduous work on the house and military service behind him, Agostino finds his footing. He decides to finish school and changes his major toward something more useful for his brewing passion: agriculture. He returns to Milan and with renewed focus completes a four-year program in three.

"Every day in Italy, we sit at the table and discuss food. We grew up with our mothers and grandmothers at the table discussing the ragu and whether it's good or not. We didn't have any beer culture. You put together the freedom to brew and this very high culture of food along with the great knowledge of taste and flavor that every

Italian has and you can do a good job as a brewer, even if you're not the very best technically speaking."

For Agostino, the technical aspect of brewing becomes the most important. He studies at various locations, including the Seibel Institute in Chicago, learning all he can.

"There's no brewing school in Italy, so I had to pick up what was available here and there. In Germany I would've been able to study brewing and it would have helped me technically, for sure. But I would've been forced towards a certain brewing school. Here I invented everything."

He does his thesis at Birreria Poretti, owned by Carlsberg, and his internship at the Von Wunster, a company owned by Heineken an hour east of Milan in Bergamo. He picks up some odd jobs in the bigger Italian brewing industry and does two brief internships at Joh Albrecht Brauhaus and Hausbrauerei Feierling in Germany.

"Then I started working on the brewery."

Chapter 5
Courting Failure

In 1994, the Bear rewrites his first, somewhat naïve, business plan in which he has calculated that if he sells forty liters of beer a day, he and his business partners will become rich. As he puts it in Massimo Acanfora's book, *La Birra Più Buona del Mondo*, "I'll leave it to whomever knows a little about the artisanal beer market to their comments."

He rehashes his business plan and pulls in eleven partners that include his brother Stefano, Maurizio Folli, Giulio Marini, other friends, and his old professor from his university, with whom he did his thesis. "My old professor was so enthusiastic about my love of beer," recalls Agostino, "he bought a share in the company."

In April 1995, they find a "suitable" location in Lurago Marinone. The building, property of the Cooperative of Agriculture and Consumption, has an antiquated aspect to it. With a building, partners, and Stefano in the kitchen, the only thing left to set up now is the brewery.

But of course, it's 1996, and Agostino, like Teo, has to find a means to comply with nonexistent or archaic laws.

"It's very strange, but you couldn't go to the local government and say, 'I want to open a small brewery,' because the conversation was:

'I'm opening a craft brewery.'
'What's a craft brewery?'
'A small brewery.'
'It doesn't exist.'"

The existing laws date back to the 1700s and require a tax man to stay at the brewery, as if he were a part of the plant. A special room needs to be set up where he can sleep and work, with a shower, bed, and toilet for his privacy.

"This meant nobody could ever open a small brewery, because the expenses from this guy would be too much. We talked with the

28

officials and asked them how we could do this. Some of them, but not all of them, were available to discuss it, to find a way. In some areas of Italy, brewers faced bigger problems with the tax people. Because laws regarding small breweries say nothing clear, everybody had to make their own decisions."

There are no regulations that state how brewers should be taxed, whether you have to pay on the wort or on the beer you sell. In short, it's a mess. An agreement is made between the brewers and the excise department. Breweries making less than 10,000 hectoliters a year are allowed to sell their beer in a pub they own, which must be close to the brewery.

"They say, 'No, you absolutely can't sell outside your brewpub. No, you absolutely can't export,' but we are. The law was, and still is, very clear because the same law rules now. We are not supposed to distribute or sell outside the brewpub."

For the moment, in 1996, some sort of law is in place. The only piece missing is the heart of the brewery: the brewing system.

"I had to design my own brewing plant. I had my ideas of what it should be. I was looking for a carpenter or a fabricator or a metal worker, but nobody trusted me. Some thought I was crazy. We had maybe one supplier for brewing equipment in all of Italy. But I wanted to do my own brewhouse. So, I finally found a man that was crazier than me and he gave me his time. We started to design the brew plant and I even helped him."

The man he finds is Ugo Paglia in Sabbioneta, a small town thirty kilometers north of Parma and two hours from Lurago Marinone. Ugo literally helps create the foundations of Italian craft beer.

Birrificio Italiano officially opens on April 3, 1996, with two beers. The first, the Rossoscura, is a dry double-malt red beer at 5.7 percent brewed with a small amount of Hallertauer Magnum hops.

His other beer is what Agostino has been perfecting since his early home-brewing days—Tipopils, the mother of all Italian pilsners.

The noted Italian beer critic Kuaska describes the Tipopils as "beautiful to look at (it can have a luscious white, creamy head) and taste, Tipopils is quite well-balanced. It has an inviting aroma of malt, fresh hops and yeast, and a dry flavor characterized by an irresistible 'bitterness' that turns into a persistent and pleasant bitterish aftertaste. It is the perfect beer to drink in only two moments of the day: at meals and between meals."

"Every beer has its story," says Agostino, "and in 1996, someone asked me, 'Why did you call it Tipopils?' The name means 'a kind of a pilsner,' something like a pilsner. I was trying to brew a German-style pilsner, but I wasn't sure it was going to turn out that way, so I called it Tipopils. It was cowardice. I took the English tradition of the final dry hopping where they put dry-hopping plugs into the cask. They do it in England, so I can do it in Italy with another kind of beer. Nowadays, few of them do it, but I knew this method, so I used this kind of dry hopping in the pilsner. In Germany they don't do this. It's against the purity law. So I took this English tradition and I put it into my pilsner. That was something interesting.

"I was and am completely free to take my own path. I had the chance to brew whatever I wanted—no respect for any rules because we don't have any rules in Italy."

Tipopils has come to define a new style of pilsner, the first original Italian beer style. Others have followed, such as Væmilia from Del Ducato, Sveva by Grado Plato, and Magut from Lambrate, all characterized by their dry hopping.

"Tipopils has been produced since April 3, 1996, and there's a very good chance it will remain the number one beer of Birrificio Italiano for a very long time."

With Birrificio Italiano open for business, a new word is added to the Italian lexicon. In Italian, *birra* means beer and the proper word *birreria* means brewery. Agostino has turned the common word *birreria* into *birrificio*, a twist that has come to mean craft brewery. In itself, the new word separates the industrial brewers from the craft or artisanal breweries. The word is commonly used today by most artisanal Italian brewers.

Everything's finally in place, except Agostino's business plan is missing one major ingredient: beer drinkers. "The problem at the beginning," he says, "was to convince people we were really brewing our own beer because we didn't have the old-style stills so many Italians associate with breweries. They didn't trust us and thought all of

this was a trick—a fraud. Some thought we were a front for laundering money. Others thought we displayed the kettles just to cheat them. An old man once told me he would never drink our beer because he knew we put water in them. Because our beer isn't pasteurized or filtered, people said we were pouring something into industrial beer to make them look hazy. We used to pour the beer in the German style, you know, two or three times to allow the head to build. The process took ten minutes and sometimes our customers would complain, and ask, 'Where are our beers?' and walk out without paying. Our beer was warmer than the standard, much warmer. Maybe the beer was too different from the standard. But I had this precise idea of the way to let people enjoy beer, no other. It was difficult."

After a year-and-a-half struggle, in 1998, Birrificio Italiano is close to bankruptcy. Agostino is forced to refinance the company. Ninety million lira ($65,000) is a lot of money. Worse, some of his partners leave. Agostino and Stefano are forced to buy their shares.

Chapter 6
Brewing a Movement

Miraculously, once Agostino's partners leave, customers start to come back asking not for a blonde or a chiara but for the Tipopils, the Bibock. In short, people in the area are becoming convinced by the tireless education being given them by Agostino, along with Maurizio, and Giulio.

"We kept on explaining the difference between the standard beer and our beer, and they finally figured out the difference was a good difference," Agostino says.

Agostino relentlessly strives to improve his beer. He gains access to better malts and hops through a new supplier in the northeast. A friend introduces him to hop growers in the Spalt area of Germany, and Agostino begins to import German hops. His beer becomes richer, tastier, and fresher. He branches out and brews other lagers, a weizen, some ales, and other "strange beers."

"I was more ambitious in the beginning. I wanted to be like Teo or maybe the best brewer in Italy or the biggest brewery, but after a few years, I liked our own pace, and very slowly, we started growing."

With customers filling Birrificio Italiano, the next challenge becomes distribution and maintaining the freshness of his beer. He begins with two-liter bottles that he fills with a very simple system he discovered in Germany. At first, he places a ten-day expiration on the beer. He soon changes to one-liter bottles and raises the expiration date to twenty days.

"What I found out quickly is my beer is better when it is fresh and fragrant since the hop aromas decline from oxidation very fast."

He is meticulous, keeping beer in his cellar from every batch bottled, refrigerating some and leaving others at room temperature. In this way, he can follow the evolution of his beer. Assured of how his beer holds up, he extends the freshness date to four months. His focus now turns to the vendors.

There is a chain of care that craft beer requires, from the brewery to the final customer, that is significant and often neglected. Artisanal beer is delicate. It's unpasteurized, sometimes re-fermented in the bottle and still alive. For craft brewers, a publican has to be a person who takes care of the beer. If the beer is not handled properly, the loss will be too great—the consumer will never take a chance on craft beer again.

"I think freshness is still a big problem in all of Italy because not all brewers follow the shelf life of their beer. Sometimes you find sour beers that are not supposed to be sour. There are bottled beers with bacteria and wild yeast that sooner or later will show themselves and turn a beer sour. If you are brewing a sour beer, it makes sense and it will probably be nice and good. But if it's just an accident, a pils or a bock or even a pale ale, sour is not what you're selling."

Many vendors are shocked and outraged when Agostino returns for his beer, kegs sometimes still full. They argue with Agostino that he is stealing the kegs, not understanding that he is there to exchange his now outdated beer.

Finally, by 2001, Agostino finds his first solid customer in Milan—a restaurant and pub. "They kept my beer in the fridge and they turned the bottles properly to maintain the freshness. With this approach, the result may have been fewer vendors, because it was difficult to handle my beer, but the vendors I had were really good ones."

Today, Agostino's beer reaches consumers with a lot of care for the fresh and full fragrance of his beer. The American importer, BUnited, the first to discover Italian craft beer, devises a clever way to export Tipopils to the United States in 2013. Agostino brews his beer without dry hopping it and places the beer in a large shipping container. Attached is a measured amount of hops. When the container arrives in the United States, BUnited dry hops the beer, then kegs it when it's ready. In this way, the Tipopils is never without its characteristic hop aroma.

"Most of the breweries in America want their IPAs or pale ales to be drunk within three or four months, maybe six months. I've been talking about this with some of my American brewing friends, like

Vinnie Cilurzo from Russian River, Matt Brynildson of Firestone Walker, and others. I know what goes on in the US, and it makes me happy because I did the same thing here in Italy. I took care of the freshness of the beer, so initially, it was an obstacle, but now it's my strength."

In trying to mimic Teo's success, early Italian craft brewers choose to bottle-condition their beer without understanding bottle-conditioning. Many brewers and publicans think bottle-conditioning is like refrigeration and will keep the beer fresh, that bottle-conditioning is the solution for any potential problem, whether microbiological or oxidative.

"If you brew an IPA and bottle-condition it," Agostino explains, "the hop aroma, which is the heart of that beer, will change very soon. It will change, probably, too much. Not everybody understands this. I still fight for freshness, but others are starting to come around."

As Agostino evolves as a brewer, Birrificio Italiano's line of beer becomes more diverse. In 1999 he begins experiments with yeasts. He develops Belgian-style beer like the Fleurette in 2001, a very light summer beer brewed with flowers.

"When I am really enthusiastic about a beer, it's usually successful. If it's a specialty beer, I won't sell a lot of it. I was surprised because we didn't expect any success from the Fleurette. It was too different from our other beers and it wasn't an easy beer for our customers to understand, but year after year, they ask for that beer, waiting even. They drink it like an aperitivo."

Agostino uses unpasteurized, raw cherries, exploiting the wild yeasts and bacteria living on the cherry skin to make sour beer, like the Scires series. He brews with spices such as cinnamon, lemon peel, cardamom, and fennel seeds—ingredients that make up today's Cinnamon Bitter Ale. With a friend who is a good, young winemaker, he experiments with grapes and their yeasts. "It can be a nice combination. I did one of my lightest beers with grapes years ago."

During his 2005 project to build a new brewery, Agostino faces his biggest challenge. There are days when he thinks about giving up and changing jobs, maybe brewing for someone else. It would be less stress, more money. He feels a little depressed and disappointed. He's fighting with his brother and fighting with his partners, and work starts to become too much of an effort, trying to do everything the right way.

"I didn't think I had done anything good."

Maurizio approaches Agostino with great energy and passion and convinces him to reconsider. "Agostino, you don't have to give up. Let's start again."

"I had to take a hard look at my life. The key for my equilibrium was to be a brewer because I had started to become more of a manager than a brewer. I realized why Birrificio Italiano was here, why it existed. Birrificio Italiano exists because I like brewing. So I went back to brewing and it changed everything. I wouldn't be here without Maurizio and Giulio. They are great pillars of the whole production."

Maurizio Folli (back), Giulio Marini (front).

Agostino finds a new building in 2011. The renovations start in September, and it's a busy period. "We worked much more than we should have. But when you do great things, this happens. My employees are passionate—all of them. Now I can relax, and that's good."

The new facility opens not far from the old location in March 2012. It's a far cry from the original cramped brewpub, now solely devoted to being a restaurant and taproom. The conference room at the new brewery overlooks the brewing area with ten taps serving guests and visitors. On the main floor is a malt storage area with a grain mill in a separate space, from which the crushed grain is sent to the brew kettle. The wort is then pumped into the next room, where the fermentation and conditioning take place. A four-step process is used to propagate the yeast. The new facility has a cooler where hops are stored, a bottling room, and a keg filler. In a walk-in cold storage area off the bottling room, bottles and kegs are conditioned and held for release. There is also an area up front where barrels are stored for future small-release sours.

Next to the conference room upstairs is a lab where the various elements of the brewing process are tested and analyzed. Agostino is the first craft brewer to have a lab from the very start. Outside, the driveway is still, today, unfinished, but more important things are happening inside. Brewing a wide range of styles, Birrificio Italiano's production grows from a two-hectoliter system (1.6 barrels or 24.8 gallons) to a twenty-hectoliter system (16 barrels).

"Our production was about 3,200 hectoliters (2,560 barrels) for 2012, and we expect a 20-30 percent growth rate to about 4,000 hectoliters (3,200 barrels). With growth, the beer becomes better, because there are more instruments to brew with."

When a young potential brewer enters the Italian craft beer world, he learns of two people right away—Teo and Agostino. They are the pillars, the forefathers, of this eclectic, rich, and still-developing movement.

"I went forward with my ideas about beer, and when you're doing something different you have to explain your philosophy, so that's what I did. It's not something I really like. But I keep doing it because I like this job. I like this job."

Chapter 7
A Young Crew with a Passion to Brew

While Agostino fights tooth and nail to cultivate beer lovers and Teo infiltrates the wine world, Birrificio Lambrate creates an entire beer scene solely through friends, the local university students, and word of mouth.

The five founders of Birrificio Lambrate—Davide, Giampaolo, Fabio, Alessandra, and Paolo—all grew up in the borough of Lambrate, east of the center of Milan. The Lambro River runs through the neighborhood and has been a significant port along the Po River for nearly a thousand years. Pliny the Elder mentions the district of Lambrate in his *Naturalis Historia* as a supply station. One of the earliest Christian chapels is found here. Lambrate was taken over by Spain in the sixteenth century, then by the Napoleonic Empire, followed by the French.

Today, the borough of Lambrate is a cluster of traffic, tight streets, and urban chaos. Parco Lambro, built in 1934, is one of the few refuges in this kinetic neighborhood. Because of its river location, the neighborhood has always maintained a list of big-name manufacturers such as the Lambratta motor scooter company.

Birrificio Lambrate starts as a whimsical idea by Davide and Giampaolo Sangiorgi's father, Franco Sangiorgi. An environmental engineer, their father often travels for work to Germany and Bel-

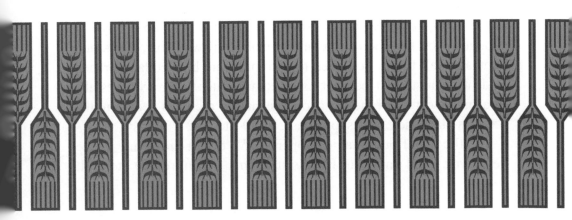

gium. Aware of the existing brewpubs there, he suggests to his sons that perhaps they should try their hand at opening a brewpub in Milan.

"We didn't even know if it was a good idea," Davide says. "We liked beer, but we had never made beer,"

Just nineteen and twenty years old and without any obvious future, Davide and Giampaolo figure, why not?

They quickly bring in their friend Fabio Brocca. Though the boys have little experience with beer, and absolutely none as far as brewing, the three young men set about making a business. They travel around Europe, particularly to Holland and Germany, to study beer and find inspiration. They become influenced by the local styles and develop new ideas. To get them started, their father buys them a fifty-liter vat, a toy in comparison to today's production. Nonetheless, Davide, Giampaolo and Fabio have a means to brew and they learn to make a couple of beers.

"We had passion," Davide says. "It started with drinking the beer, and it rolled into making it. It was just passion for making beer."

Centered between the university, the main train station, and the industrial area, the brothers' small pub, even today, is just a blip in this eclectic, electric part of the city. Stepping off the narrow Adelchi Street into the original Lambrate brewery, you enter two large doors into a courtyard surrounded by four-story apartment buildings. Kegs fill the left wall toward the back, and cars, a fork-lift, and small trucks occupy the remaining fifty-foot-by-eighty-foot space. Clothes wave in the breeze like Tibetan prayer flags from the balconies above. Behind the wall of stacked kegs are vats, boilers, hoses, and valves that make up the brewery. Here, you might find Fabio in a Left Hand Brewery fleece, toiling over kegs or bottles, or brewing beer.

In 1996, however, No. 5 Adelchi Street is just a pub barely big enough to be a fast-food restaurant. Its mahogany wood bar, stools, and booths are all tightly squeezed to accommodate blue-collar workers, students, tourists, and locals. It also accommodates the brewing vessels. In a small section of the bar about the size of a child's bedroom, the brothers place their newest purchase, a 150-liter vat.

At the small pub, magic happens. "We didn't throw any of the beer away. We'd invite our friends and drink the entire 150 liters, all in a night sometimes. It was fun. We were very young," Davide says.

They hone their skills serving a red and a light ale. People who know them come and try what they have to offer. Slowly, word spreads and more people come. Most of them are from the neighborhood. Being close to the university keeps the pub busy on weekends. As the crowds grow, the 150-liter vat can't keep up. After the pub is open only a year and a half, they need to produce more beer, and they purchase a 500-liter brew kettle. At the same time, they introduce a much more revolutionary element to their brewing: a lab.

"It was a consistent evolution," Davide remembers. "We'd brew it and drink it, and when it was over, that was it. When we looked around in the crowd, it was all people we knew. Our customers' passion became contagious and helped spur us on. They were having fun, and it was something new to them. It kept building. So we worked on the beer during the day and we really enjoyed that. Then we worked in the pub at night. But it was nice. It was a nice time."

After two years, Davide moves to build a kitchen, leaving Fabio as brewmaster, but the pub is too small to accommodate a kitchen. The kitchen, therefore, is not inside the pub, and food needs to be carried fifteen meters across the courtyard to the pub. Davide from the beginning understands that quality beer means quality food. He shops at the local market for fresh salumi and cheeses, and cooks meats and pastas with the beer wort. Sometimes he makes desserts with beer. Davide also brings in his girlfriend, Fabio's sister, Alessandra Brocca, to be the administrator of the brewery.

"Davide and I have a daughter together," Alessandra says. "We broke up but still have a good relationship. I was unemployed at the time and offered to work. I started in 1998. In 2007, they sold me a share in the company."

As word spreads, new people come. The patrons fall in love with the place, but the residential neighbors aren't as happy and complain about the noise. Packed beyond the small pub's capacity, people spill into the street outside. The police are called many times with threats to shut them down. In one incident, the police block off the entire street and close the place for the night.

Regardless, this young crew is brewing craft beer. As they begin to prosper, the businesses in the courtyard close: a cobbler, a jeans tailor, a mechanic shop. As the neighbors close shop, the brewery expands within the courtyard. The friends quickly refurbish the shops and fill them with vats, hoses, tanks, keg-cleaning lines, a bottling system, and finally, a very sophisticated lab with a true scientist, Ivo Fumagalli, at hand to work it. In 2000, they buy a ten-hectoliter (eight-barrel) brew kettle, and in 2008, they expand with a twenty-hectoliter (sixteen-barrel) brew kettle.

"When you brew your own beer and sell it in your own pub, it's easier to understand what people like, because you have a direct relationship," Alessandra says. "Some of the recipes that we had at the beginning are completely different now. When you brew by yourself and haven't had training, it's hard and it takes time to get better. Now we brew about twenty-three different kinds of beer. Eight are in our classic line that we carry all the time. We have four seasonal beers and about nine or ten specialty beers; one, the 366, is only brewed once every four years for leap year."

In December 2011, desperate to avoid being shut down and to move their ever-growing crowd away from their angry residential neighbors, Lambrate opens another pub just a few blocks from the original. Lambrate's second location is three times the size of the original pub, with a wooden bar and the typical Italian brass pour system. The kitchen this time is located inside, where Davide has an assistant. Bartending at both locations is the flamboyant Giampaolo, tall, tattooed, and with piercings, long dark hair, and a goatee. Giampaolo's energy permeates whichever pub he works with joyful energy. Just one year into the opening of the new pub, the Lambrate crew is considering opening another location, but with Italy's economic and political situation, the new pub may have to wait.

"We made a big investment in this place a year ago, so it will take time before we do something else," Alessandra says. "In December we bought a new bottling line. For some years, we've sold kegs to other pubs, restaurants, beer shops, and some wine shops, but we didn't really have a means to sell bottles. To make maybe 1,000 bottles of beer, we were working too hard, so with this new machine, we can start developing the bottle market."

You would think during this economic crisis, with such a high unemployment rate, the government would do more to encourage

The flamboyant Giampaolo.

small businesses like the artisanal breweries. Even as companies in Italy close, the number of craft breweries continues to increase—by a lot.

"It takes three or four days of work to export maybe 1,000 bottles, and three months for a response from the government!" Alessandra says. "You have to fill out so many papers, it'll make you crazy."

Even so, the Lambrate crew know they're doing something magical next to the very street they played soccer on. "I think the success of the pub is because of the local people," Alessandra says. "Now if you say Lambrate, people from America and different countries seek us out. We are very proud that we put Milan on the craft-beer map. We work every day, but we don't get to think about what we really did. It's cool to talk to other people and hear what they are doing. You exchange opinions—not just with Italians but with people from all over. It's nice, we didn't have to go find them; they found us."

Chapter 8
Glorious Moments, Interesting Times

In the early 1990s, Alessandro Borio finds himself in a tough field. The telecommunications industry is coming apart at the seams, mainly for political reasons. His brother, Enrico, and he are both well-traveled and come from a manufacturing background. They are happy doing hands-on work. In search of an industrial endeavor, the Borio brothers set out to become manufacturers themselves, except what they are going to manufacture isn't clear yet. They are passionate about cars but decide to go in the direction of the food world. The brothers are certain, at least, they are going to need good water. Turin in the early 1990s isn't going to work.

"We chose Villar Perosa because we were looking for a certain profile in the water. We grew up in Turin. The water is pumped full of chlorine there, so we couldn't use it. It's changed a little bit, but when we started, it was different."

Villar Perosa, in the Piedmont region just forty kilometers southwest of Turin, dates back to the Savoia family and was founded in 1064. As with all Italian cities, control of the land vacillated between the various dominant empires until World War II. During the war, Villar Perosa transformed from an agricultural village to a manufacturing sector.

The Borio brothers buy a large, spacious warehouse in the mid-1990s from the Sarelle train company. It's located in an isolated

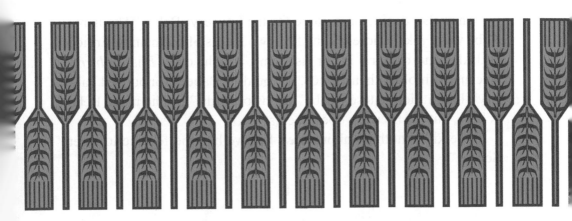

industrial zone above the village where the fresh mountain waters fill an estuary. The brothers still need to establish what industry will fill their new space, though. Both brothers like beer, and it dawns on them that making beer is a brilliant novelty. No one is making a quality beer, and there's not a quality product on the market. All that is available are industrial beers like Moretti and Peroni.

"We thought it could be done, and we began to learn," Alessandro says.

Hashing out their new concept, the brothers discuss what type of beer they should make.

"I asked Alessandro, 'What should we make?' He said, 'What are we drinking?' I responded that we were drinking this. It was a lager, so we decided to make lagers, without understanding the cycle and the base of lager fermentation and that lagers are more complicated and cost more."

The majority of craft beers in Italy are ales, for good reason. Ales spend less time in the tank, making them easier and cheaper to brew. Until 2005, their brewery is the only brewery making bottom-fermented beers in Italy. In 2013, the brothers retain the honor of being the only lager-based Italian craft brewer.

With the decision to go with lagers, the brothers learn to become brewers. They adopt the German purity law, the Reinheitsgebot, established in Bavaria in 1516, which dictates that beer can contain only water, malt, and hops.

They convert the warehouse into a pub, leaving a section for the brewery. They decide to call the brewpub Train Robber's Syndicate.

"I'd read books about South America. I worked a lot in South America between Argentina and Bolivia. It was very beautiful," Alessandro says.

They also decide on a name for the brewery: Beba. "The name Beba was a joke. These are the first two letters of our names, Enrico and Alessandro. Borio is our last name, and the other *B* is for *birra*. Because I'm older than Enrico, it would be Babe (pronounced bah-bay), but in Piemontese, 'babe' means old lady." So the name Beba is born, but the brewery doesn't exist yet.

"We knew nothing about beer. But we had the fortune to meet Scopel."

There were four microbrewers in Italy before 1996. These four were truly the first, the ancestors, opening their breweries in the early 1990s. They tried to make it against all odds, and lost. They had the courage but not the timing. These men were Pino Sposito, located in Sorrento, where he could take advantage of the American beer drinkers from the US military bases in the Campania region; Orabraü, owned by two brothers in the town of Torbole on Lago di Garda; Aramini Alessandria, who owned the Tortona in Turin; and Adias Scopel, who was from the Veneto region but opened his location in Cagliari on the island of Sardegna, where he worked many years for Heineken as head brewer. These were the men Enrico and Alessandro would come to emulate, but they were all short-lived ventures.

The customs and excise taxes were a mess and for the two brothers at Lago Di Garda and for Orabraü, it just became too much, so they eventually closed. Sposito died, and Scopel left his brewery to his grandson. Sadly, Scopel's grandson preferred the beach to work, and the brewery closed. But Scopel lived on.

He was one of the few who wrote on his Italian identification card "Brewer" for profession. He had earned a degree as a brewer at the Feltre School, an educational institute that taught master brewing. Feltre's brewing school eventually closed "like everything does in Italy." Scopel went to Germany to do his internship.

He became head of production for HB in Germany, then went to Heineken-Cagliari. In Cagliari, Heineken was run by a family who worked closely with their in-laws. The in-laws started putting friends and relatives in top positions, and this didn't set well with Scopel. Unable to get along with the family, Scopel decided to quit and open a brewery of his own. He was from the beer industry, and he leaned heavily on his contacts from Peroni, particularly his brother who worked for Peroni as head of production in Pelusa, near Rome.

"Scopel is sixty-five years old today," says Enrico. "We're talking about a long time ago. He is a true master brewer, unlike us. We learned as we went and are self-taught. But Scopel had the education. In the beginning, Scopel would tell us about things we'd never heard of."

Scopel is a godsend to the brothers. Still in need of equipment, they are handed the first designs for a small brewing plant from Scopel. It is basically a Heineken plant shrunk down to fit their needs.

"We had nothing, so we explained what we wanted, and the Heineken people, Scopel and his producers, designed it to our scale," Enrico says. As a miniaturized industrial plant, the brew plant has all the whistles and bells of a high-tech industrial plant. "There were knobs that fell off, and we left them because we didn't really need them. When labels fall off, we don't replace them. I don't even know what this knob does; we've never used it. In the back, we have valves we've never used."

Beba's miniaturized industrial system.
Enrico Borio explains how lost knobs were never replaced.

Now that they have a building, a name, and the equipment in place, the brothers search for materials. Once again, Scopel steps in. The first malts they buy come from Scopel's brother at Peroni.

"Scopel's brother did us a favor. But we kind of got sidetracked using alternative Swiss, Italian, and French malts," Enrico says.

"I remember the first time we heard from a supplier for the barley," says Alessandro. "I explained to them that we were a small producer and would they like to work with us. They said, 'Of course, how many silos do you have?' In my mind, I was saying, 'Silos ... for the malt?' I explained, 'No, not silos, sacks.' The guy on the other end became indignant. 'Sacks?! You dimwit, it's been thirty-eight years since we sold bagged malt.' Some suppliers simply thought we were playing a prank on them and whenever we called, they often hung up."

Eventually, they find the German malt they need to make German-style beer. The correct hops take a while to source. It's a long process, but most of the work is in isolating the yeast. "It's not a yeast that can be found on the market. It's a mix of lager yeasts. This was probably the most important work," Alessandro says.

With everything in place in 1995, the brothers are ready to start brewing. Scopel helps and teaches the brothers how to weigh, measure, and follow the rigors of brewing.

The first time the tax people come to do their inspection, they have no idea what they are looking at. The brothers lose six months tangled in the bureaucratic process. The health department takes their samples of beer, which of course are still fermenting in the bottle, to their labs for analysis and end up leaving them on the desk for two months. When the official from the health department contacts the brothers about their beer, he says to them, "It looks like mud, not beer." On the verge of having their product marked unsafe and undrinkable, the brothers rush in to save their future. They explain to the inspectors that this beer isn't like Peroni or Moretti, which can be left on a shelf for two months and won't change at all because it's dead material: Their product is more like cheese; it's still alive.

The official decides to try again. He writes in his first report, "We didn't finish an analysis of this product because we don't know what it is."

The brothers give the health inspectors samples again and explain to them that if the inspectors are not going to do the analysis that day or the next, they should please put the beer in the fridge.

Finally, with approval in hand, the brothers take another two or three years to solidify their recipe.

"It's much more difficult to make simple beer. I don't like beers that are too aromatic, too rich. I can only drink so much of it. They're too aggressive for me, and even if they are well made, they don't appeal to me. We like the more sophisticated beers, the beer without spices and without fanfare," Alessandro says.

"We are for a product that doesn't have to shock you," says Enrico. "At first it surprises you, then what? Our beer lends itself to be drunk. Today it's probably easier to start off with solid recipes, but not back then. We didn't have anywhere to go. There was no Internet."

The brothers continue to seek Scopel's help when they have some doubts, sending him samples and asking his opinion. Even when Scopel responds that the beer is good, Alessandro remains worried. "He'd say, 'Relax, what more do you want to do?' He was a big help for us," Alessandro says.

Brewing is all an adventure, a new discovery for the brothers. They learn with the marvel of children bemoaning that they can't see what's going on inside the fermenters. "This stuff, why does it turn into beer?" Alessandro wonders.

The first lager recipe they brew is appropriately called Number One. The 4.8 percent lager becomes the number-one seller, making up 50 percent of their sales. Their other thirteen labels make up the other half. A very simple lager, the Number One is a beer you drink amongst friends. "It's our Tipopils. It's our thread," says Enrico.

Their second beer is a doppio malto called La Toro. Translated, *doppio malto* means double malt, but in technical terms, it's more akin to Belgian designations of dubbel, trippel, quadrupel, telling the consumer that this product has more malt character, not necessarily double the malt. La Toro pays homage to the Juventus fans and the historical location of the famous soccer team who practice just up the road. The word *toro* means bull, the symbol of Turin, which, in Italian, Torino, means "little bull."

"We're here for the water," Alessandro says, "not for the team, but we have to name things. When a client wants something easy to drink, we give them the lighter beer, and when they want a little more flavor, we give them this one. It's the philosophy we've followed for many years. Now we have some beers that are more complicated and take more time because they require more technical skill."

With their beer in place, the brothers bring a specialty to their kitchen to match the originality of their beer: the gofri, a Piedmont Valley tradition. The gofri originates from the early communion wafers with the symbolic rosary in the middle. The waffle iron that made the religious hosts dates back to the 1200s, left behind by pilgrims who passed through the Pillar Valley on their way to visit the pope in Rome. The poor stuffed the gofri with leftover pieces of pig. The wafer, made of water and flour, was used in place of bread. Today, the Borio brothers use the common Italian sandwich fillers of cheese, prosciutto, mushrooms, and such.

Alessandro (left) and Enrico (right) Borio with their famous gofri.

With the kitchen in place and their beers coming together, the brothers have taken their first steps to becoming Beba, yet Italians don't understand. Beer is not in the base of their culture. The brothers face their wary countrymen's uninformed scrutiny and accusations of boiling the beer.

"They were like, 'You're buying it and selling it like it's yours'. It was very difficult in the beginning because they didn't believe us. So we'd take them to the back and show them. They'd ask, 'What are those?'

"'That's where we make the beer,' we'd say, and they would respond, 'No, I don't believe you.' But little by little as we spoke of artisanal beer, we found listeners who were more accepting." Alessandro explains.

"The first years, the beers, the parties, the events, everybody drunk, you can imagine—they were glorious moments, interesting times," Enrico says.

Chapter 9
Keeping It Small, in a Big Way

The experience of building Beba brings the brothers to a sobering reality. The idea of becoming big is put aside. "We stopped expanding because you take €500 and you throw it into the brewing vat, then it's a million, then that's not enough. I don't want to invest millions of euro into things to make things. We know the math very well. We work at the maximum technical abilities of the cantina—that's it," Alessandro says.

The brothers are content in 2013 with their size of their brewery and the beer they make. It is a recipe that keeps Beba moving forward. Their only big purchase is two maturation tanks, which help them in the high season—lagers just take too long. They eventually hire a man to help in the back. Although times might be less glorious and the imagination tempered, the focus today is on quality, but in many of the new breweries, the brothers are finding an ingredient that leaves a bad taste in their mouth—marketing. They prefer to be validated by the content, what's inside the bottle, not what's on the outside.

"According to me," Enrico says, "it's not correct that an artisan needs to spend millions of euro to do his profession—an artisan shouldn't have a department of marketing. But this is a discussion that nobody wants to talk about. I bust my ass producing in solitude beers that are balanced, that are good, that satisfy the clients. I am getting the best out of the technology that I have over there in the brewhouse, the best. According to me, the small artisanal brewery has the aspirations of the territory, the justification of a market from their territory."

Until recently in Villar Perosa, the brothers remained the outsiders, the ball busters from Turin. As the main road bends and twists itself out of town, you are quickly in the middle of nowhere, and that's where you'll find the Train Robber's Syndicate. There are no shops, stores, or even sidewalks. It's an industrial area with warehouses and without tourists. The Beba road sign blew down a few years ago. When the brothers found out the cost to repair it, they decided to leave it down.

"We felt if you want to meet us, you'll find us. And if you find us because you sought us, then I don't have to explain things to you," Alessandro says.

Without a sign, a newcomer simply has to guess where the brewery is. You take the graveled path down the hill, around a typical prefab construction office along a chain link fence to the brewery on the right. All the shops and factories are closed during the hours of the brewpub's operation. There's no neon light, sign, or patio, but once you enter what seems to be an office door and see the wooden tables and chairs, the taps on the left, and the large brewing machines, you'll know you're home. And the brothers will make sure you feel that way, too.

For the first ten years, the brothers eked out a hardscrabble life selling to the local pizzerias and beer stores. Today, the brothers contract brew a few beers outside their own labels. They bottle 80,000 bottles a year and export Beba beer to various countries around the world. But that doesn't mean that they've softened their stance against industrial products.

They are inclined to make special beer for special occasions. For their tenth anniversary, they made a recipe that was 10 percent, symbolizing their ten years in business. At Christmas, they brew a stronger winter beer. For their spring beer, called Talco, they brew a white lager representing the color of the graphite that was once mined in these parts. To celebrate their love of cars, they brew a very dark beer called Motor Oil.

"We were a little drunk with the guy from BiDu, Beppe Vento, at a festival, and he says to us, 'You two gnomes, could you make an ale?'"

"So we said sure. We squashed two teasers at once by making a top fermented beer, added spices, and then we called it Two Gnomes (Due Gnomi) to make fun of our small stature," Alessandro says.

Like their old friend Agostino, the brothers believe in brewing a drinkable product, not so much in beer for pairing with food.

"We're more of a beer of the bordello. Beer is more for parties. It's not beer for tiny cups. We're about beer drinking," Alessandro says.

No longer worried about the return on their investments because everything is already paid for, they don't go chasing after styles. This is their beer, this is what they do. They make the money they need, and that's good enough for them.

Chapter 10
Lessons in Frustration

In fifteen years, the Italian craft-beer market already has all the structure, all the evolution it took wine 500 years to build, but it lacks a unifying body. For the entire Italian craft-beer industry, the greatest impediment to continued success is the Italian government. Excessive taxes and the absence of uniform national rules stifle the growth of the craft brewing industry while the lack of a national association to represent the breweries aggravates the problem. For old and new, this privation of unity renders craft brewers victims to the whims of the government. In essence, Italian brewers brew under regulatory warfare.

Lorenzo "Kuaska" Dabove (left) with Luca Giaccone (right).

"The most important thing about taxes and beer is the complexity of the tax system," says the beer writer Luca Giaccone, author of the *Guide to Italian Beer*. "The brewers spend tons of hours working on their taxes. We need national rules that are simple and easy to follow."

"It's living hell," says Alex Liberati, founder of Revelation Cat Brewing in Rome. "You're doing everything yourself. You're brewing in the morning, running to the customs office in the afternoon, speaking with the exporter at night, and if there's one little problem with the form, you're done. Recently, there was a problem where a guy wrote Birra Artigianale on his label and he got fined €10,000. He's a craft brewer and he got fined for writing Craft Beer on his labels because, technically, you're saying this beer is better than the other ones. It's crazy."

Anytime someone is forced to deal with an Italian clerk at a bureaucratic office, it's like heading to the playground to deal with the bully. "I know a lot of breweries that began to brew six months to

Revelation Cat taps at Brasserie 4:20 in Rome.

a year later than planned because they couldn't get their permits," says Luca Giaccone. "They have everything ready. They're paying for the brewing system, they're paying the rent on the building, they have their raw materials; everything is ready, but they're waiting on a stamp from some useless state employee. Recently, a brewery in Lombard went to court to denounce an official who asked for a bribe to get the stamp to brew. They filmed everything, filed charges, and weeks later, they had permission to brew, and that official is now in jail. I hope things will change, but at this moment, we're in the middle ages."

"These impediments come from old laws that matured over centuries," says Renzo Losi, founder of Panil Brewing near Parma. "Why the Italian government doesn't help, I'm not capable of answering. They impede you from working. A delinquent is more privileged than a brewer."

What laws exist today date back to the reign of Maria Theresa, the Habsburg monarch of the mid-eighteenth century, when northern Italy was ruled by the Austrian Empire. Little has been done to update them. The laws suit the industrial brewers, but they were never designed to address the concerns of small brewers, particularly craft brewers.

"Until 1995, the law said beer had to contain at least 50 percent rice or corn," Alex Liberati says.

"In my case," says Mike Murphy, founder of the defunct Rome Brewing Company, "I had an Ufficio Tecnico di Finanze (UTF) officer who dealt with Peroni, and they were kind of baffled about my case because I was so small. The UTF is the tax-enforcement branch. They were real methodical about watching us. The worst thing about it was how much work they made the brewer do. Every UTF office is different. One place might do it this way, but if you're up north and they're dealing with a lot of wineries, they might treat you a little differently.

"I had to keep a registry of every kilogram of malt I had, that I purchased and that I used. If I didn't use it and I had to destroy it, I had to get documentation that I destroyed it. Same with the hops, and they counted my water use too," remembers Murphy. "I had to make all of these logs. There were like five different registers written by hand. I had to send a fax to the UTF office every time I was brewing, telling them I was brewing. I had a two-hour window, and I had to tell them if something came up and I had to stop. They kept tabs on what I did, and once a year, they showed up and pretty much lived in the office all day going through all the registers, adding up all the flow meters, looking for any discrepancies in the recording. It was awful."

"You have to act as a warehouse, which has a fiscal deposit," Alex Liberati says, "which means you're not paying taxes on the beer unless you release it from the warehouse. That means you're keeping government taxes. And when you keep the government's money, they're weird about how you keep it, so they're knocking on your door every week. And every week, there's a fine. I went through it, and it was horrendous.

"So, what happened, to get the small brewers not to do this, they created an exception that said you could pay as you go. You produce this amount today and that's what you pay for. The pay-as-you-go thing says it's not paying on your end production, but it's paying on the sugar content in the beer when it passes through the heat exchanger, before it goes into the fermenter. But this means you can't do things like dry hopping. You lose 200 liters of beer when you dry hop, but you've already paid taxes on that beer, so that means it's more expensive to dry hop. But that way, I don't have to have a fiscal-control audit every week and I don't have to keep an insane calculation of every bottle I produce."

"From the beer inside the fermenter," says Luca Giaccone, "to the one placed inside a small 33-centiliter bottle, a 750-millileter bottle and a 1.5-liter bottle; for the state, that's three different products with three different codes and three different excise taxes—one beer, three different bottles, three documents. It's absurd."

Beer is one of the most controlled substances in Italy, and the system lumbers on. "I went to the government office and wasted a day after I sent them an e-mail," says Fausto Marenco, cofounder of Maltus Faber Brewery. "I had to physically go there and tell them everything I said in the e-mail. In Italy, bureaucracy is a job and it requires bureaucracy to maintain it. It's the first industry of Italy."

"When you export, the excise in Europe has to be paid in the state where it's consumed," says Alex Liberati. "When you ship the beer, you ship it with two documents. One gets stamped and sent back to Italy when the guy in, say, England gets the beer. With that document, you go to the state and say this is how much I shipped; it wasn't served here in Italy, so give me back the taxes I already paid. That doesn't happen. It happens in every other country, but it doesn't happen in Italy. If you want your taxes back, you have to go to the tax office and battle for it and maybe you don't have to pay taxes on the next batch you brew. You have to do this every time."

If Italy really wants the craft-beer movement to grow, the taxes have to be equitable to those of wine.

"The only fermented beverage that pays tax on alcohol is beer," says Alex Liberati. "Wine doesn't. Anything that is not made with barley isn't beer, so it doesn't pay tax. But we do."

"We are going to see a 30 percent raise in our taxes over the next year and a half," says Agostino Arioli, cofounder of Birrificio Italiano, "while the wine industry got none. Wineries have books where they write the wine movements in and out of the warehouse, and they have columns where they should write down the tax they have to pay, but they always write zero, because they pay no taxes. They have the papers, but they always write zero. It's ridiculous."

"In the 1980s, there was this beer-import boom from Belgium," says Alex Liberati. "The wine industry got worried because no one had seen beers at 10–12 percent. The wine lobby said, 'You've got to protect us, we're a wine country, you've gotta protect us.' So the government agreed, 'You don't pay taxes.' Why? Because everyone who's a politician in this country has a winery, so they don't pay taxes."

For the Italian brewers to be heard they will have to approach the government as one voice, by way of an association. Going it alone won't bring them closer to success. When a company tries legislating on its own, it can be perceived as promoting a particular brand or doing things in a way that a certain brewery does it. Only with an independent, collective voice can the Italian craft brewers succeed in convincing the government that Italian craft beer is really making an impact. It's a growing market that draws tourists, creates revenue, and provides employment. That message should be easily conveyed and received in a struggling economy, but this is Italy. They could take a look at another burgeoning craft-beer scene, the one in England.

The brewing industry in England suffered a foreign takeover in the 1980s and 1990s. The vast majority of pubs became tied houses, contractually locked in with their big-brewery owners, which didn't allow room for small, independent breweries. For the most part, small brewers in England went out of existence. About five years ago, the government allowed a tax break to small brewers. Since then, hundreds of new breweries have opened.

"England wouldn't have had that opportunity unless they got the tax reduced," says Charlie Papazian, founder of the Brewer's Association in the United States. "You just can't compete when, as an example, MillerCoors is buying their hops for $2.50 a pound and you have to buy it for $20 a pound. You can't compete."

In the United States, craft brewers unite under one umbrella, the Brewer's Association. This unity gives a single tiny brewery a much bigger voice when it comes to lobbying Congress and turning the heads of its members toward the jobs, tax dollars, and constituents affected by their decisions. The work of the Brewer's Association is threefold: to promote, to protect, and to provide access to data.

The Italian government is blind to the bigger picture because there isn't a cohesive group collecting information. Data collection is probably the most valuable tool the Brewer's Association provides for its members. Information is power. By collecting numbers on what is being produced, what is being sold, how many are being employed, the association provides brewers with information that becomes a tool of empowerment when presented to a government official or elected representative. It reveals the most coveted number of all to a politician—constituents.

"Promoting is fundamental and essential to any organization, while protecting is almost a no-brainer. It's good for business," Charlie Papazian says, "to keep a rein on regulations and pay fewer taxes. That just hits your bottom line."

This is necessary if Italian craft brewers want to implement changes. Working together as a group would encourage allied trade in the people who want to sell equipment, supplies, technology, and consultation, who all have lobbies of their own. In the end, they will partially fund the organization, too. With an organized collective, a future can be mapped out, sketched in so people can see the plan on how, as a group, they will move together.

"We don't have the group power like the Brewer's Association in the US, and so we are where we are now," Alessandro Borio of Birra Beba says.

"One source," Papazian says. "The breweries have to get the ball rolling."

Chapter 11
Let's Get Together

Italy's oldest association, Unionbirrai (Brewer's Union), was started by happenstance in 1997.

"The association began when Guido Taraschi, of Centrale Della Birra, called a supplier to find a hydrometer," says Alessandro Borio, cofounder of Birra Beba. "The supplier responded that someone else had already asked for one and he didn't have any. Guido realized if someone else was looking for a hydrometer, then that someone must be brewing beer like he was, so he looked into it and found us."

"Then the same thing happened with a winemaker," says Enrico Borio, cofounder of Birra Beba. "We asked for some part and the winemaker responded, 'Some other guy asked us too, some guy from Cuneo.' We were able to get the information, and we called Teo Musso. We were like, where are you? Piozzo? I'm sorry, I don't know where you are."

Eventually, Guido, Alessandro, Enrico, Agostino, Teo, and the crew from Lambrate find each other. Further to the east in 1997, Stefano Sausa opens his new brewpub called Vecchio Birraio in Padua. Guido suggests they all meet and see what they can do together. The owners of the six breweries decide to meet in Vicenza at the chamber of commerce. "So we found each other," says Enrico Borio. "When we built Unionbirrai, the first motive was to meet each other."

This hodgepodge of innovators form an association originally called Unionbirra. The name is quickly changed to Unionbirrai because a beer club is already using Unionbirra. So, a small group has been created that will try to change the laws for microbreweries, to set standards, and, more importantly in 1997, to share ideas.

In 1997, brewers are forced to travel abroad if they have questions about brewing because there are few, if any, resources and no books in Italian about brewing. Most of their equipment is fabricated from scratch because Italy has no market for small breweries. Much of what they need requires some serious searching. Coming together allows them a great opportunity to connect their resources. Not long after launching the association, Italy's craft brewing pioneers find they aren't alone.

"Those were the best years," recalls Alessandro Borio of Birra Beba, "because we were building everything,"

After only a year and a half, however, cracks begin to appear. Stefano is the first to take himself out.

"He may have already understood it wasn't going anywhere," Alessandro says.

Today, Stefano Sausa brews 500 hectoliters (400 barrels) at Vecchio Birraio, where he bottles what he wants and sells them at his small location in Padua.

Not long after Stefano leaves, Guido divorces his wife. Realizing his ex-wife now owns Centrale Della Birra and is going to profit from his beer, Guido quits. Eventually, he returns to the movement, but not as a brewer—as the president of Unionbirrai. The pioneers continue to interact through their new association, organizing beer tastings and giving each other a hand in the perilous virgin waters of the Italian craft-beer scene—but the active fault that lies underneath Unionbirrai is far deeper than divorces and taxation.

"One of our regrets is we weren't able to build a strong group," Enrico Borio says. "Italy has remained a nation of bell towers. There is little attention to the collective."

It's a fundamental cultural divisiveness, a mistrust of one another that has been brewing for millenia. Next to the Italian tax system, regionalism, known in Italian as *Campanilismo*, or bell tower-ism, is the greatest challenge for the nascent movement.

"In Italy we don't work well together," says Luca Giaccone. "We have a long history where we developed a unique state from twenty different states. We have the Vatican, Tuscany, Liguria, Piedmont, every one of them with a different language and not too long ago, one hundred years or so, different money. Italy is a country where you travel one hundred kilometers and you don't understand the language. The dialect changes completely. The food is completely different from one region to another. Everything is different. So, we have this problem, and I think, with regards to beer, that problem will always exist."

Campanilismo is a term that expresses the intense Italian regionalism. *Campanile* in Italian means bell tower. Each town had its own church with a bell tower that sounded off, not only the hour, but when farmers were to be out in the fields, when it was time to return for lunch, when it was time to end the day. The bell tower also rang when the town was in peril due to fire, or if there was an oncoming invader. In its time, the bell tower was as essential as our cell phones are today.

The entire town and the broader close-knit communities subsisted by way of their church bell towers. In turn, they came to represent the people, the people's town, the people's community. Italians are, in essence, their bell towers. It's a rare moment for Italians to call themselves "Italian." In general, Italians introduce themselves as Romani, Vicentini, or Milanesi if they're from anywhere close to these major cities; otherwise, they will refer to the province: Liguria, Lazio, Campania. Even more deeply, an Italian might consider himself brethren not to other Italians but rather to the ancient Etruscans, Lombards, or Romans before Italian.

"You cross a river and one side hates the other side. I went to the first beer festivals we had here and they were already fighting," says Renzo Losi. "Agostino, who was the vice president of Unionbirrai at the time, was already fighting a lot. This was like 2001."

"I have to admit I was fighting for my point of view," Agostino Arioli, of Birrificio Italiano, says. "But I think, honestly, every man should. If you have a dream, you should push for it. So I pushed a lot. My dream was to have not the brewers-lobbying association, but to have the craft-beer community association. The American Brewer's Association was born like this. I thought home brewers, professionals, and beer drinkers all wanted the same things: good beer at the right price, emotions, and fun. There's no reason to be split into different groups, because we're working for the same thing. I still think it would be best to be all together."

"At some point we started getting irritated," says Enrico Borio. "In 2005, there were 180 producers in Italy and we found only about twenty-five were in Unionbirrai. We invited all of them to Bologna.

Only thirty-two showed up, of which twenty-four were already in the association. After that trip, we left Unionbirrai to its own path."

The mega-industrialized breweries of Moretti and Peroni aren't really the craft brewer's Goliath. It's the Italian government that they must take on to survive, and doing so regionally isn't enough. "It's very difficult to work together in Italy," says Bruno Carilli of Toccalmatto Brewery, located in north-central Italy. "Two years ago, I tried to found a brewers association. We had a meeting with twenty-five brewers and we agreed about a lot of different things, but after two days we didn't. We have Assobirra, which represents the industrial breweries, but I don't have the same interests as Peroni. At the same time, I can't have the same interest as a home brewer."

"The problem with Assobirra is they are multinationals, not Italian breweries. Their goals are completely different than ours," says Agostino Arioli. "It's true, they are fighting for lower taxes, but we're fighting for a different goal. Our goal is to have a lower tax than *them*."

"Where I have to put fifty people in my brewery, a big industrial brewery can use one, due to automation," Teo Musso says. "You can't compete with that. We'll never compete with the big breweries. A small brewery can make specialty beer and quality beer, but they can't make beer for the masses. They make a beer that's bought and shared by five people in a pub—they're not selling five beers, they're selling one. We're the beer of Sundays. People who buy a $15 beer are an entirely different concept than people buying a six-pack of Heineken. It's a completely different market."

"Mixing with the big breweries is simply ridiculous," says Agostino. "It only serves to confuse everybody about what is craft beer and what is, generally speaking, called beer. My colleagues who paid to join Assobirra were dreaming about special benefits. They thought the majors would help them, but they got nothing—no more than they got from Unionbirrai, and probably much less."

"We have to let go of the idea that artisanal brewers need to grow to do anything in the market," Teo Musso says. "An artisanal brewer can only send out an artisanal message."

While Unionbirrai struggles, sharp divisions continue to exist on how to define an artisanal brewery. According to its website, Unionbirrai defines an artisanal brewery as "a brewer who produces unpasteurized beer in establishments that do not reach quantities exceeding 5,000 hectoliters per year."

"In Italy, our movement is small enough that we can still have this argument about what 'artisanal' means," Teo Musso says. "To me, 50,000 hectoliters is the right threshold to still be considered artisanal. Certainly, there will be someone in this tsunami that will go over that number.

"There has to be a person behind it. I don't see if you make one million barrels that there's a person behind it anymore. They could be great producers making exceptional beer, but it brings into question the message. It has to be a live product; otherwise, don't put artisanal on the label. If it's been filtered, it's not artisanal anymore. I'm pushing for laws that define what it means to be an artisanal brewer."

"It doesn't matter whether your beer is alive or pasteurized or filtered or made at 50 hectoliters a year or 10,000 hectoliters a year," Charlie Papazian says. "If you want to get something done, you have to work together and not criticize each other's beer. The craft brewers need a plan that can eventually have an influence on the government for regulations. You want to create an image for all Italian craft beer. Maybe you don't even get into the definition of what is an artisanal brewery. You don't do that until year ten. Just say small brewery, don't even put a cap on it."

Because Italian craft brewers haven't found a way to present themselves as a group, every brewery is defining for itself what an artisanal brewery is. Thus, to the consumer, they're communicating one artisanal beer brand at a time. With more than 600 breweries and more coming, this means there will be many different stories being told, which could ultimately confuse the consumer.

"If the big brewers come out with a really good, tasty pale ale or a rose hips, wine-infused beer, what's the difference?" Papazian asks. "The consumer's going to say, 'What the hell? Why am I paying for expensive craft beer? I'm going to drink that other stuff.'"

Without a definitive answer to what an artisanal beer is, the consumer may just as well assume artisanal beer doesn't exist.

"The industrial brewers want to exploit the successful name of Italian craft beer and mix the two," Agostino explains, "because industrial beer in Italy is not successful at all. Craft beer is successful in Italy, but they have never been. We should be stronger and better defined before we merge with the majors."

Though Unionbirrai may struggle to keep a united front, it continues to provide consultation and directives that simplify taxes, and it does this well. Unionbirrai organizes courses, tastings, and beer events. It keeps members updated via its extensive internet site and publishes a quarterly magazine called *Unionbirrai News*. It also retains important domestic and international relationships in the beer field. The union advises professional brewers and beer entrepreneurs on regulations and helps them manage and create purchasing groups. The organization also provides courses for aspiring entrepreneurs or breweries in operation.

"All things considered," Agostino says, "Unionbirrai is doing a good job. Today, there are eighty breweries in the association and the proposals are well thought out. They provide courses for people who want to open a brewery. It's very effective. Things would've been much worse without all the things Unionbirrai is doing, and used to do."

Unionbirrai organizes the Beer of the Year, the Pianeta Birra Festival, and the Salone Del Gusto with Slow Foods, venues that allow small brewers to showcase their beer and to have direct contact with their customers. Unionbirrai's biggest success has been to get the Italian government to recognize small producers. The government now defines a brewery brewing less than 10,000 hectoliters per year as a small producer.

"The fact that they recognize us is a huge positive result," explains Alessandro Borio.

"Government and taxes are a problem in Italy," says Agostino, "but despite this, we're growing, and growing fast. Birrificio Italiano is brewing 35 percent more than last year. Many of my colleagues are growing at this rate. They are successful. Of course, we could grow faster with help from the government, but it's not bad."

Chapter 12
Something Wild

Headed by Lorenzo Losi and his sister Patrizia, Panil looks beyond Italy's borders for success.

"I'm working with exporters almost exclusively," explains Patrizia Losi. "I'm even sending Panil beer to Brazil and Canada. At this point, I have to. If I wasn't exporting, I'd be in a lot of trouble. Italy's in a lot of trouble right now. We're growing, but there are a lot of people jumping in, and all the new breweries will choke it up. We were the ninth or tenth craft brewery in Italy. You invest a lot of money in this with few rewards."

While the pioneers have had four years to hone their brews and build an association, in 2000 the son of a winemaker in Parma embraces the wild and makes sours.

"I like wine, but from when I was about fourteen years old, I drank beer seriously and I always liked Belgian beer," Renzo Losi says. "I liked Trappists and the sours. Because we're close to Belgium, England, and Germany, they were our influences. There are two different schools here. Agostino is more German and Teo is more Belgian, but that stuff depends on your personality. You like this or you like that."

"It's unusual for a winemaker to turn to making beer," says Patrizia. "We don't make wine anymore. My dad used to make wine."

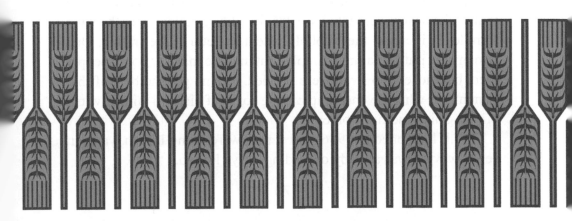

The Losi family has been making Lambrusco wine for four generations, dating back to the 1930s. Parma is steeped in culinary history, home of some of the world's most recognized Italian products: prosciutto, parmesan cheese, cream, milk, and, of course, wine.

In 2000, Renzo is one of very few brewers outside Belgium spontaneously fermenting beers, a radical idea anywhere in the craft-beer world. There are a handful of US breweries making small quantities of sour beer. Sours are just as foreign in the United States as they are in 2000 in Italy.

"In the beginning, it was like talking with Martians," Patrizia explains. "I tried to get the locals to try our sours, but they wouldn't drink them—not even for free. We couldn't give it away. The Italian consumer is not open to a lot of diversity in beer. The forty-five hectoliters of the old Barbera reserve that we set aside will make more than 40,000 bottles. I'd be happy selling all of it in the US, because selling it here is very difficult. Maybe two out of ten Italians drink sour beers."

Renzo Losi is something of a wild scientist. At the age of twelve, Renzo is already a home brewer serious about brewing beer—so much so that he persuades his wine family to embark on a new adventure as artisanal brewers. It's a crazy idea, but the family will eventually take that chance.

"Vineyards still believe they are the most important in the industry and that won't change, ever," says Renzo. "But it's already been thirty years since Italian wine has gone to shit. They were already adding water to their wines back then."

By Italian law, each year, a certain percentage of the wine production is sent to the state to be rated. A value is assigned to the wine based on the amount of alcohol it contains. Up to twenty Italian winemakers were convicted in 1986 for adding methanol to the wine samples to increase the alcohol content to get a higher rating. One winemaker put his tainted samples out into the market. Some people died, but those who lived were blinded. Karma got the best of that winemaker when he ended up buying some of his own tainted wine, blinding him and his mother.

"This happened in 1986, and if they were doing it then, you can see how wine was already degrading," says Renzo.

Renzo Losi, founder and brewer of Panil.

After Renzo finishes university in Bologna, he sets up a space in their winery and in 2000 begins brewing. Infusing his beer with enology, Renzo is one of the first in Italy to use champagne yeast to ferment his beer. But his most radical concept, not only for Italy but for any country outside of Belgium, is to utilize spontaneous fermentation.

With a deep understanding of his land, Parma, one of the richest lands in Italy, where world-famous cheeses, milks, hams, and much more fill the air with a bonanza of wild yeasts, Renzo aims to capture his territory in the most fundamental way. He goes as far as cultivating wild hops that grow well in Parma's rich, fertile soil. With his beer, La Divina, Renzo experiments by fermenting in the spring and then in the fall to see what variations the wild yeasts provide with the different seasons.

Renzo's not afraid to experiment. He takes chances and has to dump more beer than any beer lover would care to know, but if that's what it takes to make sophisticated and taste-enhancing beers, then that's what Renzo will do. With his Black Oak beer, Renzo cuts oak barrels in half to allow the beer to spontaneously ferment in the open air.

The beer Renzo brews most, however, is a blonde, La Bionda. "It's not easy to make a blonde, then turn around and do a spontaneous.

You're always in danger of contamination. You're always cleaning. I have to vaporize at a hundred degrees. If there's any misstep, you are in trouble."

In essence, Renzo brews within a cesspool of wild yeast and bacteria ready to pounce on his live, clean beer that is not meant to be soured. And he's doing it to perfection. This is Renzo Losi's mad, mad lab. And he works his beers flawlessly.

"Making a beer that isn't acidic is unthinkable, because the whole brewery is contaminated with this wild yeast and bacteria," explains Andrea Lui, Panil's new brewer.

As it is the brewer's nature to be meticulous, Renzo steam cleans every inch twice, to be sure. The results are a light, very clean Belgian-style blonde. Renzo's unique beers take full advantage of every aspect of the land, from air, to earth, to Parma's naturally clean water.

"The Bionda is the one I made the most of because it was the one I could produce in more volume. It pleased me very much to send my beer to the US, but what really displeased me was selling so little in my home area. It was very sad for me. You need to have a different mentality in order to drink beer. I fought a lot with my family about that—for me, what interested me the most was to sell in my location."

Working with his family is sort of like his beer—bittersweet. "Not too long ago I was thinking about wine," Renzo says. "It's been written in paragraphs here and there that there's more arrogance attached to wine, because people feel more sophisticated and of a higher class. But beer needs to be respected. We're struggling to get people to understand that beer can be just as sophisticated. Italian beers are good, well made. Italy takes a lot of care with food and beer. This clash with wine is very important. I don't know, maybe wine is more important to the Italian, but it has to be integrated. In

Italy, the breweries clash with the wine culture. I had clashes with my father that eventually made me leave."

On April 25, 2012, on Italy's Liberation Day, a national holiday celebrating the Allied troops' liberation of Italy from Nazi occupation, Renzo Losi walks out on his family, his brewery, and his legacy.

"My brother left the brewery last year," recalls Patrizia, "and suddenly we found ourselves without a brewer. He left because of family issues. He wanted to leave. I put out a want ad, and Andrea answered."

"I've known Renzo for twenty years," says Andrea Lui. "I had some books at home and did some research. I never collaborated with him on a beer. All the recipes are Renzo's with minor adjustments. For now we have to satisfy our orders. Tomorrow, I don't know, maybe we will study something else and develop new beers."

Panil's future now lies in Patrizia and Andrea's hands. How they will fare with a near-total export concept remains to be seen, but the Panil beer dating from 2013 are the last ones Renzo produced there. Where he has disappeared to, no one in the Italian beer world knows. Renzo simply has dropped out of circulation. Wherever he went, Renzo made his mark.

GRADO PLATO

Chapter 13
A Fine Joke

When Renzo Losi was home-brewing beer in his teens, Gabriele Ormea was only a toddler. The year Agostino and Teo opened their breweries, Gabriele was twelve. By the time Gabriele opens Birrificio Grado Plato in 2002, Gabriele is merely nineteen years old and the owner of one of the earliest brewpubs in Italy.

At the end of 2001, Gabriele finds a headline in the town newspaper, *Orario di Chieri*: "Giving Away Liquor License." To open a pub in 2001 requires buying one of the few existing pub licenses. There are only five in Chieri, a small town in northwestern Italy about seven miles southeast of Torino that dates back to the Neolithic and Iron Age.

For laughs, Gabriele and his brother send a business plan as a joke. The concept they file is for a brewpub/pizzeria or a sports bar, or a combination of the two. They were just going to jump into the market with this idea of a small brewpub.

That evening, the boys contemplate calling to apologize for their tasteless joke and asking if they could pull their plan. Instead, their father, Sergio, convinces Gabriele to follow through. To qualify to win, the contestants must have the means to fund their plan. The men go to the bank to apply for a loan. Getting a loan in Italy is as difficult as obtaining citizenship in the United States, but destiny is on

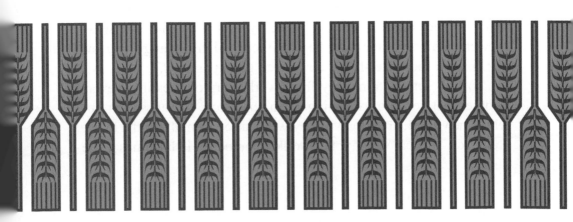

Sergio and Gabriele's side. Earlier that week, the old, hardened director of the bank was replaced by a younger woman, new to her position. Without much thought, she approves their loan. "We were flabbergasted. It was incredible; there was this thing that was happening to us," recalls Gabriele.

To open a brewery requires the usual health inspections and navigating the notorious tax laws, but with the turnkey pub license in hand, Grado Plato is spared the most agonizing hurdle. The name Grado Plato translated means "degree plato," plato being the way Europeans tend to measure the amount of fermentable sugars in the beer wort before fermentation begins.

"We decided to open as a brewpub with two beers: a light and an amber," says Gabriele. "We felt like pioneers. There were breweries open before us, but there were so few."

Gabriele's most incredible fortune is his father, who is one of the few Italians home brewing. "He's my teacher, he's a brewer. I was very lucky. We traveled by train to breweries to drink beer and returned home with our backpacks full of beer."

Unlike Renzo's and Teo's fathers, who are deep in the wine world, Gabriele's father, Sergio, like Giampaolo and Davide's father, Franco, is the first generation to have access to foreign beer. In the 1970s, beer from England, Germany, and Belgium were making their first strong presence in Italy. Young men like Sergio and Franco were venturing toward different tastes, and liking them. In turn, they passed this influence on to their sons.

"When we opened, I was nineteen years old and my dad was more than fifty," explains Gabriele. "For thirty years, he worked on the highway as a toll-booth attendant. Up until 2010 he did two jobs: he worked at the brewery and did his job on the highway. Not a job that he liked at all. In fact, it probably frustrated him. He was a brewer, but not just a brewer; he was interested in farming and growing his own food. He always developed great passions."

To find satisfaction away from work, Sergio dives into several hobbies that become something of an obsession. He takes them to a whole new level, creating whiskey with barley he malts in the house. He makes grappa, wine, potato vodka, and beer. He becomes a beekeeper.

Gabriele Ormea, the young protégé brewer.

"I didn't care for any of his passions, but for beer, I did. I was six when I had my first taste of beer. It was a type of brown ale, almost opaque and not really clean. It had a big, creamy, yellow head. It had notes of almost raw cereal. I don't know if that's exactly the truth— maybe I'm just convinced of the story now—but when I have beer, I remember it. After that taste, I was like, *dong!*"

By the time Gabriele reaches high school, he's devoted to beer, wondering if a Torino kid can get a job in this ambiguous field. Sergio and Gabriele home brew a few beers together. In high school, to make a few bucks, Gabriele takes a job as a bartender. "So I had already begun to pick up this trade."

The very first recipes for the new pub come out of practicality; inspiration comes later. Sergio and Gabriele understand that simple beer will be easier to explain to their beer-ignorant clients. "It's not like we took off with great beer," Gabriele says. "We wouldn't even recognize our old beer today. Explaining artisanal beer to a client was hard."

The first tool of communication is the pub. In Italy, a brewer has to reason with his clientele in small steps. A brewer doesn't sell his first batch; he sells the second. The first batch is solely to prepare the grounds so the second batch then has an audience. The more brewers educate their patrons, the more opportunities they have to sell.

In a short time, word spreads about this artisanal brewery in Chieri. As more people come, Grado Plato slowly begins to provide work and benefits to the local economy. The staff has to learn how to present and serve beer, how to describe the beers and pair them with food. Grado Plato is deeply committed to beer and food together; the kitchen and the beer are one. For the staff, suggesting pairings is an essential part of the job.

"We did a lot of tastings, even inviting Kuaska to explain the beer, with someone else to explain the food."

The main course at Grado Plato? Snails. The Durante snail is served with seasonal asparagus from Torino—some of the best in Italy—and also with a pasta made with tomatoes and basil. Beer is often an ingredient used to caramelize onions or used in the Savoia cheese, which is fried together with three beers. Grado Plato makes bread and pizza dough from its beer. The Lardelatte snails are served with local peppers that Sergio discovered and had to have on the menu. Their first course includes a risotto with mint and speck, a smoked prosciutto, as well as pasta with sausage ragu. They make a pasta alla carbonara, but instead of the traditional cream sauce, they use an asparagus béchamel.

Samples of the amazing food served at Grado Plato, including their famous snails.

"It's fun, and we feel like it's part of our work to cultivate this food. What's in style right now in Italy are itinerary tastings being held by a wine taster and a beer taster. They go from restaurant to restaurant and serve beer, wine, and food with a piece of paper to score it. Beer wins 90–100 percent of the time. They're doing this all over Italy. The floral aromas in beer open a whole topography in food that you can't necessarily pair well with wine. Wine flavors make only a quarter of the way around a circle of choices, while beer completes the whole circle."

Not long after its start, Grado Plato begins to veer away from the simple light and amber beers. Because of Agostino's renowned Tipopils, making an Italian pilsner in Italy is nearly an obligation. Grado Plato's pilsner, the Sveva, represents 70 percent of sales during Grado Plato's first four years.

"Sveva is our Tipopils. It's clean in the mouth, light, low-alcohol—it's like water," says Gabriele.

Because Italians have had experience with ambers, the amber becomes Grado Plato's second biggest seller.

"In the beginning, the styles we chose felt necessary," explains Gabriele.

During a vacation to Corsica, Gabriele spends an entire day brewing at the Pieta Brewery. From that trip, Gabriele comes back with the idea to do a chestnut beer. "My father, being interested in farming and being a beekeeper, had to make a mead, so we made a chestnut, honey beer." This becomes Grado Plato's fourth beer in two years.

Two-thousand and five is the year Gabriele sets himself apart from all other brewers and brings the Italian craft-beer world into full circle. "We had this idea to make an autonomous beer, all from one area. From the earth to the glass, with malts and hops made by us. We worked with the Institute of Agrario Vittone di Chieri, the University of Asti, and the Institute of Bonafous-Città of Torino. Utilizing the agricultural center of the Institute of Bonafous-Città the students collaborated to grow hops and malt. It was fantastic. We had these young people making local malt and hops."

As the materials are being cultivated, the beer hasn't quite come to fruition, so they explain their project to Kuaska. Without hesitation, Kuaska suggests they make a sticke.

"I said, 'What the fuck is a sticke?'"

A sticke is a variation of the traditional Dusseldorf altbier, but darker and stronger. It was invented by the Uerige brewpub of Dusseldorf.

Sergio sets off to Dusseldorf and returns with a case of beer. "And then we went back to grab more. We thought, 'Okay we can make this beer.' We brewed 1,000 liters as an experimental batch and decided to call it the Sticher [pronounced sticker]. It's called Sticher, marrying the German name sticke with the local dialect 'cher'" which refers to Chieri, so it's Sticher."

It takes them two years to develop the hops alone. Three years after they began the program, Kuaska comes to try the Sticher.

"It was very emotional, presenting this beer," says Gabriele.

When Kuaska tastes the Sticher, his reaction is straightforward: "Wow, I'm taking you to the Great British Beer Festival."

"For us, that was when it changed. That was August 2006. It was our first step into the international beer world."

That year, Jean Van Roy, the great brewer at Cantillion, visits. "What an honor. It was him, the brewer from Rochefort, and Eric Wallace from Left Hand Brewery in Longmont, Colorado, who all came for dinner. Teo, Luca Giaccone, and Kuaska were here also. We served them all snails. How beautiful."

Beer after beer, Gabriele produces outstanding products that not only hit their mark but set their own standards. "We began to win some small prizes in Italy, and we began to have more courage."

One night as Gabriele returns home late, he finds his father sitting and waiting at the table. "I was dead tired, and as soon as I walk in, he assaults me. 'You know what I just saw? I saw this documentary about the American invasion of Sicily during World War II and the American soldiers were giving away chocolates to the children. The Sicilian children had no idea what chocolate was. They had the rubica, which is a very, very sweet black fava bean that was played off as a chocolate. With the American invasion, the Sicilian children discovered what chocolate really was. They ate it like horses.' When my dad saw this, it was over. We sat down and had a few beers and spent all night discussing this. That night, the Chocarrubica was born."

The name Chocarrubica pays homage to *choca*, "chocolate," and *rubica*, the Sicilian fava bean that was a chocolate substitute made for the poor. The most important thing about the Chocarrubica is the line of malts, which give a conceptual taste of chocolate, bringing out the creaminess of chocolate, and a great density to the beer with a texture of yogurt, thick and fatty.The chocolate is provided by a Piedmont master chocolatier.

Gabriele is only twenty-two years old when the Chocarrubica is created.

By 2007, Sergio and Gabriele begin to make a living and are sought out by L'Assosazione Burnett, a distributor. From this point, Grado Plato begins to sell beer to pubs.

Gabriele reaches a milestone when he is interviewed by Evan Rail from the *New York Times* for his 2008 article "Savoring Italy, One Beer at a Time."

"One day the lady from the hotel next door said to me, 'All these people are coming to see you. What the hell do they want to talk to you about?'"

While Gabriele is at work in 2010, Luca Giaccone, the beer writer and judge, calls Sergio from France to give him some news.

"I was working a lot at the time," recalls Gabrielle. "I was at the Salone Del Gusto and went home for an hour to sleep before going back to the pub. My dad calls while I'm asleep and says, 'We won the World Cup.' I said, 'Who? Juventus?' and I hung up."

What they won was platinum, the highest prize at the Modial De Biére in Strasbourg, France, for the Chocarrubica. This was the equivalent of Ghana winning the World Cup.

"That was a crazy, amazing thing for an Italian beer to win."

When Grado Plato opened in 2003, there were only four brewpubs in Piedmont. By 2012, there are more than seventy. Artisanal beer drinkers from all over Italy and around the world are coming to Cheiri.

"The current generation finally understands the concept. What I enjoy and love is when my friends get married, they ask me, as a gift, to bring beer. So I bring them beer in a jockey box. When I see the grandfather and the father, that generation that only drinks wine, and they're not drinking wine at the wedding, but instead drinking beer—that gives me great pleasure. In this way, we're building culture."

Chapter 14
How to Build a Ferrari

For Riccardo Franzosi of Montegioco Brewery, it's not about building culture so much as returning to its roots. Montegioco recedes into the region and embraces *campanalismo*. For Riccardo, Italy is a big country, not a nation.

Nestled in the foothills of the Liguria Apennines north of Genova, Montegioco is surrounded by the southern tip of the Piedmont region, a stone's throw from the Lombard and Emilia Romagna borders. In this valley, one pasta is called agnolotti; in the next valley over, it's called ravioli. From trattoria, to restaurant, to family home, a soup varies. One place may add peppers while another uses tomatoes. Every house has its own recipe. "Which is why I laugh at recipe books," says Riccardo.

Riccardo's story begins with a search for a new path in life.

"I worked in a whole different industry, in construction, working for my family's business. It was an independent company that saw big growth, and at some point, I realized this wasn't what I wanted. Thirty-five years into it, I thought, 'This is it?' I wanted to do something that was mine."

When Riccardo was drinking beer in the 1980s, he wasn't thinking about brewing. "I liked beer, but I wasn't a fanatic. If I had a choice between a good wine and a good beer, I'd choose the beer."

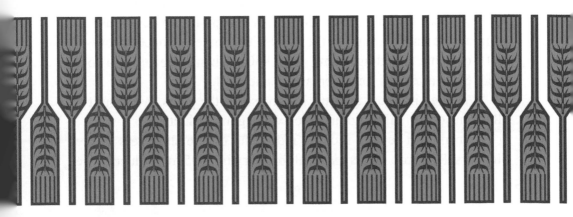

It's about ten years later when Riccardo really digs in. He inquires about beer and seeks out Teo Musso at Baladin.

"I would go to Teo's to drink these beers, and they were delicious. I found that I liked the Belgian styles. The first beer I tasted where I realized it was different was a Westmalle Tripel. When I drank it, I said, 'Huh?' But generally, if I have a choice between a good pilsner or a good blonde, I'll choose the blonde. Maybe because it comes from the wine, the fruit, not just the acidity, but there's a fullness in the mouth—the composition."

Going to Teo and Agostino for direction, he becomes aware of how the pioneers are brewing their own beer and figures he can do this too. "The initiative wasn't for the beer. For me, it was a path, to do things the way you see them in your head. To want to make a product the way you like it. I saw how they made beer. I tried them and drank them. And from there the idea came that it might be possible to put the two together—change my life and make craft beer."

Many of Riccardo's recipes come from when he was home brewing. Although his friends are his first critics, he has the great fortune to meet Kuaska, who assists him early on. With guidance, Riccardo refines his home-brewed beer until Kuaska suggests that he make his move to becoming a professional brewer. Riccardo has his doubts. "I had a job. It was a big risk."

At the end of the 1990s, Riccardo retires from the family business, and in 2000, he works toward this idea. His family isn't very happy about it.

Riccardo starts by rebuilding—not his beers, but the plant. The building was built originally by his grandfather in the 1930s for grain storage. It's located on family land along the main road that winds through the hills and orchards of the Apennines. The old granary is across the street from the family compound. After its use as a granary, it was a theater. In the 1970s, it becomes a house of love—well, of cattle breeding—until the 1980s, when it becomes a tool shed. Soon after, it's forgotten and abandoned.

"I cleared it all out and just left the shell, the posts. We rebuilt it all. Some of it's still original. Then we began production."

Armed with several recipes and riding on the shoulders of the pioneers, Riccardo opens his small brewery in 2005 to produce some of the highest quality beer in the country, utilizing the fruits of his fertile Grue Valley.

"It seemed completely natural to tie the beer I made to the land. The ancients used the materials around them to ferment. Tombs were found in Liguria dating back before the Celts with amphorae filled with barley and grapes mixed together. Before, there was no distinction between wine and beer—if it fermented, it fermented."

Riccardo Fanzosi.

Out in the country, the air is full of wildflowers that bring each season in with their own unique scent. Using what is at his disposal in a valley where peaches, grapes, and strawberries grow, Riccardo embraces materials that have been utilized for generations. Over time, Riccardo develops them into magnificent and uniquely Italian craft beer. "I'm tied to the region," he says.

By exploiting the unique peaches found nearby in Volpedo, Riccardo develops La Quarta Runa, perhaps one of the most spectacular beers. Not just in the Italian craft-beer world, this beer stands out on its own in any craft-beer country.

The peaches are cooked without their pits into a kind of jelly, then added to the base Belgian blonde beer for two weeks. The key to the Quarta Runa is in the peaches themselves. Cooking the more mature peach, rather than the younger ones used in jam, allows the taste of fruit to push through.

The Quarta Runa has an intense nose of ripe peach, but without the jammy finish in the mouth, by utilizing hop bitterness to finish the flavor. Often, a peach beer is too sweet, but the Quarta Runa is dry, sublime, and beautiful in its simplicity.

Sam Calagione from Dogfish Head Brewery, in Delaware, while at the Salone Del Gusto, compared his peach Berliner weiss, Festina Péche, to Riccardo's Quarta Runa: "I made this beer like a limousine, but Riccardo's is a Ferrari."

"It reminds me of the part of the peach that's right next to the pit. When you first bite into a peach, it's sweet, but as you get closer to the pit, it gets a little more bitter," says Riccardo.

It takes Riccardo four years to develop the Quarta Runa. Riccardo has to wait for the peaches to return each year, and every harvest, the peaches are different, like wine. "We just have one shot and that's it."

Riccardo represents the artisanal man. He left the big industry for the country life, returning to his land, taking time, not to build numbers for a bottom line but to build a great beer. The Quarta Runa's subtle brilliance rivals that of Saison Du Pont or Russian River's Redemption. It takes a richly experienced beer drinker to understand how expertly this beer is made. There's nothing to hide behind. Any flaw would be readily evident. If Riccardo represents the artisanal man, then the Quarta Runa embodies *campanalismo*'s best attributes by using *his* land's peaches.

"This gives me a lot of satisfaction, not just from a sales standpoint, but because they are products from here. You have to create something that's yours. When you drink this beer, you say, Montegioco."

Riccardo's idea is to develop and expand a little at a time so he can give the best service to his clients. Working alone in the first year, he produces about 150 hectoliters. None of his products are able to be made on request. Many take three years or so to develop, because many of Montegioco's beers are barrel-aged. Several Montegioco beers exported by BUnited will be out in 2015–2016 and they're already spoken for in 2013.

"Saying it like that makes it sound like a big deal, but it's a small amount."

In the beginning, Riccardo tries to coordinate his timing to the orders, but he soon decides against it. Over time, his clients become willing to wait. It's worth it, they say.

"They might come to buy a particular beer and I might be out, so they say, 'Okay, we'll get something else,'" Riccardo explains.

Even Matthias Neidhart, owner of BUnited, expresses his willingness to wait.

"We haven't had any problems so far with exporting," says Riccardo, "because I wait for the beer to mature. I have friends that brew to sell. They bottle their beer to be shipped, and they have problems. It's too warm, it doesn't ferment. I wait until the beer is ready.

"I have to admit Matthias was a very important person," Riccardo says. "I can only speak well of him. I was very lucky. It happens that you run into these people in the trade that are very aggressive, but it didn't happen to me."

It's not that Riccardo just ran into incredible people by chance; he met people who wanted to join him. He was never interested in mass producing. Montegioco only produces 500 hectoliters annually. Even Eataly, the huge, ever-expanding Italian market chain, accepted Riccardo's limitations and agreed to take his beer whenever it's available. "We have a saying here: There's more time than life."

It's a breath of fresh air that people can still respect time in this hustle-and-bustle world of industrialized globalization, but they can only do this if the product is good.

Riccardo says, "My job is to make a good beer. They help me do all the rest so I can focus on the beer. If you try to fulfill orders at a certain number of liters, eventually, you're going to fail your product. For instance, I can only make the Quarta Runa when the peaches are ripe. And I can only get the peaches in July and August, then I put the beer in the barrels when it's cold. I have to wait three winters for it to finish. If you want something every week, go somewhere else. I choose to do things this way."

Riccardo is convinced that the modern idea that a company needs to grow infinitely is fundamentally wrong. "Normally, you do these things to launch yourself toward bigger things, but it's not in my nature. My heart's more in the work. In my opinion, you don't have to invest big in order to relax. I don't need the stress.

"I was asked by the American market if I could do Quarta Runa faster, so I tried a different peach. It had more acidity and less sugar. After six months, it lost all its sweetness and only tasted acidic. If I make good beer, how come I need to make more? It's good! First it's ten, then fifty, then a thousand, then a million.... It's infinite. I've had offers to grow the company, but I'm not interested. You start out going home at five, then it's six, then after dinner. If twenty-four hours isn't enough to do your job, then the problem isn't your job, it's you. We started out at this size, and this is how big it will remain."

From the very beginning, Riccardo's product is well cared for and well made, cultivated from the moment it begins to boil, all the way to the bottle. He labels his barrel-aged beers *metodo cadrega*, an old wine term in which *cadrega* means chair and refers to sitting and waiting for the slow, natural maturation in the barrel. Through word of mouth, his beer is sold mainly to restaurants. He starts with the blonde, the Rat Weizen, then develops the Demon Hunter, which is a strong ale. Eventually, the Quarta Runa makes it on the list, deriving from a home brewing recipe, followed by the Drago and the Brante.

From the beginning, his sales are good. The people who buy his beer return. "We still sell to the people who first bought our beer."

You know immediately that the bottles, wrapped in beautifully colored paper, are from Montegioco. Each label has a unique story with quirky images laced with symbolism.

On the Runa bottle, a rock with an X chiseled on it represents a transformation, not just physical, but toward death. Riccardo translates this to his beer as representing things lost that can't be eaten that are then transferred into the beer.

"When you're drunk, you make these things up," he says.

The label for the Rurale depicts a shovel, which is a symbol of hard work and physical labor in the fields, with a crow, an ancient symbol, on top because it can travel between the world of the dead and the living. The person standing in overalls, barefoot in the field, is a portrait of a friend who is known as a local guru and custodian of the rural life. He often walks around without shoes, maybe wearing them two months out of the year. The crow defecates on the shovel, "Which symbolizes you work, you work, you work, but in the end, what does it mean?"

Riccardo won Unionbirrai's prestigious Brewer of the Year award for 2012.

"I believe artisanal came before capitalism and it will exist after. The world of artisanal gave birth to capitalism."

For Riccardo, artisanal is about the land, the countryside, his home. "I was born here, and I'm tied to the region. I think it's much

Montegioco's paper wrapped bottles.

easier when you work with small numbers. It's more human. It's always about the quality. When you speak of trust, quality is always the foundation. You put a face with your client, especially with beer that is high priced. It has to be justified. You're obligated to give absolute quality."

Chapter 15
The Malt Smith

Some of the elders of Genoa remember the smell of malt in the air from a brewery called Cervisia, a brewery that employed 500 people until the mid-1970s. Cervisia was bought by Heineken, who closed it.

Today, the smell of cereal from wet malt hangs in the air again at the old brewery, but the men brewing here today, Fausto Marenco and Massimo Versaci, come to this fateful juncture through a more contemporary method: home brewing. Both are ex-employees of the dairy giant Parmalat at the Central Milk Plant of Genoa. Massimo worked in marketing, and Fausto worked in the lab.

"I was quality-control officer for Parmalat in Genoa and had a pretty high-up job with a lot of responsibilities with a lot of complaints and few compliments," says Fausto.

What bonds the men to their destiny is their love for beer. Fausto tests the waters as a home brewer in 2000. He continues until 2002, when he meets Massimo.

It's during a trip to Bamberg, Germany, that Massimo finds his passion for beer. One night, at the Irish pub Minou Risso, Massimo meets fellow Genovese Kuaska. The two immediately strike up a passionate conversation about beer, of course. By night's end, the idea to bring beer aficionados together gives birth to La Compagnia della Birra.

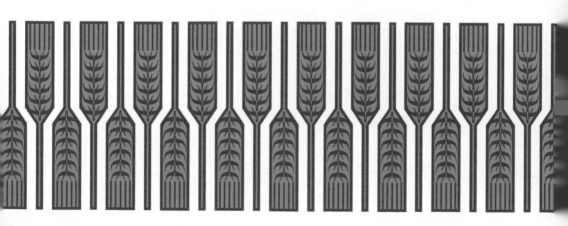

"It's a cultural association. With Kuaska, we set up trips to Belgium; we did it for fun," says Massimo.

Massimo sets off to bring his region of Liguria, his home of Genoa, to the table in the form of local cuisine to introduce beers. More importantly, Massimo launches a very successful home-brewing program. Soon after, Massimo and Fausto meet and in 2003 build a 200-liter vat at the cultural association as their own private brewery. After nearly sixty batches, it's clear to friends and fellow beer-loving associates that Fausto has the touch.

"We entered a contest where there were forty international judges, and we finished second in all of Italy with our Extra Brune. We thought at that point, good things are happening; the way things are going, we can open a brewery. One would brew and one would promote it," Massimo says.

"Massimo does the commercial stuff, the communication, the beer tastings. I'm the brewer. Massimo is more of a personable guy. I'm more reserved." Fausto explains jokingly, "If a beautiful woman comes in, he'll tell her, 'No, Fausto isn't here. Can I help you?'"

The two fuse into a positive force, and a friend tags them with a name: Maltus Faber, Latin for malt smith.

After finding the historic location, they remain unable to find a brewing system that satisfies them, so Massimo and Fausto build their own.

"We knew what we wanted," explains Massimo. "We designed everything. We designed a sleeve around the vat that keeps it cool, and this saves energy and money. We designed this, and many other Italian breweries copied it."

The two men open Maltus Faber at the site of the old Cervisia brewery in 2007, exactly one hundred years after the original brewery began in 1907.

"We're lucky because we're in a kind of quiet place, and that's very hard to find here in Genoa," Fausto says.

Under the competent hands of Fausto, the faber begins to work his skills on the maltus. When they begin, the dominant influence in Italy is Baladin, known for its Belgian-style approach and use of exotic spices. Fausto eschews spices and brews with a concentration on the malt, water, hops, and yeast, like the Germans. So successful

Maltus Faber's self-designed brew system.

are the two men at brewing German-style beer, an article about them and their beer is written in a German brewing newspaper.

"We were able to produce something in Italy different from the normal," says Fausto.

When giving tours of the brewery, Massimo and Fausto pass around covered plastic dishes with malts inside "because most people don't know what malt is." Using American, English, and Belgian grains, Fausto creates softness and texture and bends his beers toward unexpected flavors. Because they are already well versed in brewing, it's not surprising that their beer is to the level that exporters and distributors are already waiting at their door: "Even before we opened, there were distributors and importers seeking us out. We immediately started exporting with BUnited. We send 200 crates of beer to Japan every year. Some go to Monte Carlo and Austria.

"The hard part is to make the beer and then sell it. A privilege we have, like Montegioco, is that clients look for us; we don't have to look for them. If you opened now, it would be harder for people to find you. If your problem is that your product is being requested and you don't have enough, well, that's a good problem. Today, we just labeled a product that's still aging and we've already sold it. For now, that's great, but that's not always guaranteed," says Fausto.

Having spent so many years teaching at their association, the two men find education a fundamental part of Maltus Faber. They don't snub people who are ignorant about beer. It's more important to reach out to those who don't know the products than to just be there for the judges and the journalists.

The downfall in Italy is a lot of food traditions, none of which include beer. Penetrating this cultural vault, Maltus Faber introduces beer to the table as a guest of the food. "We really want to bring beer to the food," says Massimo. "What we do to get people to taste these quality beers is to present them with quality foods and have them think about what would go well with them. Italians understand food, but they're skeptical about pairing it with beer."

Aware of how the Italian mind connects beer with pizza, Massimo sets up a tasting called Every Beer for Every Pizza. This long association of beer and pizza derives from the crafty marketing of industrial breweries many years back. The big breweries saw that one of the only common foods from north to south was pizza. The idea to sell beer in pizzerias was a move to get their products sold across all regions. That connection continues to exist throughout the country.

"*The* beer doesn't exist; there are many beers. Just like pizza, there isn't just one, there are many. It's a different approach to the material. In this way, they're eating something familiar and we get them to try a familiar pairing with an unfamiliar form of beer," says Massimo.

Relying heavily on word of mouth, the duo travels often, introducing their beer across Italy and Europe. Even so, Maltus Faber, like the Borio brothers at Beba, rely on local sales, selling to bars and restaurants close to home. For them, this is artisan.

"We do an artisanal distribution," says Massimo.

Maltus Faber is not pretentious. There's no store or fancy shop at the brewery; you pretty much drive up and buy beer. The space feels more like a machine shop, with its high ceilings, stone walls, and cement floors. Everything is stacked high because there's not much room. Vats, boilers, tanks, catwalks, kegs, and bottles are all crammed into a 200-foot-by-200-foot space. The lab is a sliver of space, and a nook serves as the bathroom.

"We have to be like that. In our reality, that's the only way we can work. We're tiny," says Fausto.

The duo is in no way presumptuous, either. They are very clear about the path they want to take. They brew three beers every twenty days, brewing every other week. This year, they'll brew about sixty beers, totaling 60,000 to 64,000 liters (500 barrels). When they're not brewing, they're bottling.

"We made about 500 hectoliters (400 barrels) last year," Fausto says.

In the artisanal debate, size does matter. While Teo believes in numbers no more than 50,000 hectoliters (40,000 barrels) to remain artisanal, Beba believes a brewer can't remain artisanal past 5,000 hectoliters (4,000 barrels). For Maltus Faber, it's very important to not get too big; to Massimo and Fausto, each bottle is full of quality and time. Massimo and Fausto are more interested in selling two beers to someone knowledgeable, then a third to someone who is just attracted to a blue bottle or nice labels. In the end, what matters is the product inside.

For the Italian craft brewer, this concept of remaining small is as much a qualitative argument as an economic one. Taking a €200,000 loan early on, today, Massimo and Fausto own everything in their brewery, something they are very proud of. They don't plan to buy anything anytime soon, because they don't feel the need to grow.

It's not that Maltus Faber doesn't want to grow but that it can't grow. Exponential growth may work for Baladin, but it won't work for Maltus Faber. "We make ales, so we don't have a cooler. It's not necessary for these types of beers. But if we wish to improve the quality of our beer, we need to buy a cooler. We try to invest conscientiously, so if we get a €15,000 cooler, it's a lot of money, but it's a good investment because we have to invest in better quality," says Fausto.

Massimo and Fausto just bought a warehouse and plan to open up space in the cramped historical brewery and renovate the crumbling stone floors. This is a key investment for them, allowing the

Memorabilia from the Cervisia brewery.

current area to be just for production. In Genoa, there's not a lot of room. The entire city is smashed between the sea and the mountains. The city is built on stilts that raise highways above grottoes, homes, and businesses. The extra room will gain Maltus Faber another one hundred liters. A few modifications, more time, and more practice are the main focus for Maltus Faber.

"If you tried our beer two years ago, you'd find they are better now. They've evolved. That should be obligatory for an artisanal brewer, because if I tell you I make a lot of beer and I distribute it around the world, but it's not good, then it's the end of the discussion," says Fausto.

Maltus Faber tries very hard to sell directly to its retailers. The two men believe this is key to their future, because a distributor will never sell their beer the way they want, never have the same care for their product. Fausto and Massimo are looking for people who will care about their product, and this takes time.

"We were one of those who opened just early enough. Now it's harder to open a brewery. I think our market will be more fragmented in the future," says Fausto.

At the dawn of the movement, passion was perhaps enough to get a brewery started. The breweries opening in the second wave are mainly home brewers who connect through associations and clubs, but the future breweries will be opened more and more by experienced brewers who've brewed at known breweries.

"There are two things, according to me, you can't buy today: time and experience," says Fausto.

Those who just take advantage of the moment and try to jump in with the wave aren't going to succeed. "It's not like if I see someone make furniture, I can just go and make furniture," says Fausto.

Until now, Maltus Faber has forged ahead. It's a system that works for Massimo and Fausto. "Just a few months ago, this became our only profession," says Fausto. "At first, it was just weekends, then a few days, and then more days. We're at cost; we're not making any money. We do it for passion. We work twenty-hour days sometimes. We have a more direct product, but it's not banal. Five years from now, I don't think we'll be much different. But I hope my beer is just a little bit better."

Chapter 16
The Bigger Picture

By 2007, the Italian craft-beer movement has become very different from that of 1996. With materials such as specialty malt being bagged, with hops readily obtainable from all over the world, with multiple smiths able to make brewing equipment, the Italian craft-beer movement is well underway. Although the government still lags behind, craft brewing is no longer a foreign concept. Bureaucratic blueprints for taxing and managing small breweries are available, and though they continue to vary wildly from region to region, they do exist.

The cultural landscape has also shifted in the movement's first decade. Dotted with associations and clubs, home brewing, beer tastings, and national contests are becoming more commonplace. By this point, if someone is seeking craft beer in Italy, they'll find it. Though Italian craft beer still remains minimal, its growth has led the movement to greater national exposure, and it has begun to make its presence felt internationally.

Many of the next generation of brewers start out home brewing and connecting with the various breweries in their local areas. They head to Piozzo, Lurago Marinone, Lambrate, and Villar Perosa to seek advice, suggestions, and, in some cases, even apprenticeships with the pioneers. Many of the new brewers are opening with an eye

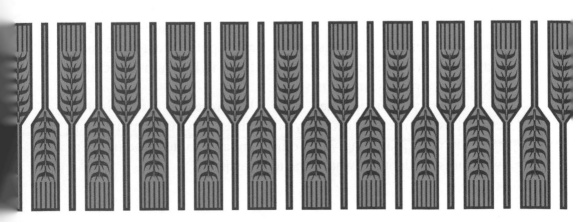

on the greater business picture, recognizing the swelling wave of growth and expansion. Nobody exemplifies this better than Giovanni Campari.

Giovanni grows up in a world of learned people. His parents are educators. His father is a professor of film criticism and film history at the University of Parma, while his mother teaches Italian literature. She is also an entrepreneur. For twenty years, she runs a small company that organizes cultural events.

"In my family, I have always been surrounded by scientists, mostly medical doctors, but since an early age, I was also exposed to art and culture," says Giovanni.

Giovanni is poised to become part of the Italian craft-beer story through his longtime fascination with fermented foods and beverages. While studying food science and technology at the University of Parma in 2004, Giovanni experiments with home brewing.

"I started home brewing with an all-grain method, and with very bad results," says Giovanni. "But I realized I had found my calling. I decided to dedicate myself to quality and excellence. The first time I tried a good craft beer, it was a revelation. I said to myself, 'I can't go back.' You say to yourself, 'I deserve more. Life's too short.'"

Brewing allows Giovanni to express himself in a way that wine-making can't. He recognizes wine as the expression of the land while beer is more an expression of the brewer.

"Of course, we are a wine-oriented country, because of our culture," observes Giovanni. "A craft brewer in Italy is like a wine maker in Germany. Germany has fantastic wine makers because they aren't oppressed by tradition."

Making beer isn't just a craft of measured materials but an interaction with who Giovani is. Given all the variables in beer making, he appreciates the infinite range with which he can manifest his creative side. Beer-making is his canvas, and he puts his emotions into each beer with a passion and dedication that will lead him to become Italy's most award-winning brewer.

"I am truly fulfilled when, after a long research, I can finally 'taste' those same emotions in my pint of beer," says Giovanni. "And it is even more gratifying when others are able to describe in their own words the depth of what I wanted to express."

Before he's able to express his artistry, Giovanni apprentices himself to an old master quite adept at expressing himself through his beers, Agostino Arioli, brewmaster at Birrificio Italiano.

The enthusiastic and dedicated Giovanni couldn't have found a better mentor. Under the tutelage of Agostino, a man whose main ingredient is his soul, Giovanni studies the man as much as he studies the craft. Agostino's wisdom doesn't end with brewing, and the main lesson he provides Giovanni becomes an ingredient not included on the recipe.

"I was fascinated by the man more than the brewer. His philosophical approach to life was something I really admired, something that is very much reflected in his beer."

Guided by his creativity, Giovanni focuses on managing and controlling the variables of the process. He comes to understand the importance of being comfortable with the equipment, like a painter with his brushes. In the end, Giovanni realizes that home brewing is much more difficult than brewing professionally.

To get Giovanni started, Agostino sells him one of his own early vats. Giovanni finds a building not far from his home in the small town of Roncole Verdi, close to Parma in the north-central region of Italy called Emilia-Romagna. Roncole Verdi is famous for being the birthplace of the renowned Italian composer Giuseppe Verdi. It's also known for its prosciutto, as well as its wines, Lambrusco and Malvasia. In 2007, with this historical backdrop, armed with a new vat, a list of recipes, and christened by one of the great originators, Giovanni adds one more ingredient to his future success: his business partner. While Giovanni is the visionary brewmaster, Manuel Piccoli is the brewery's entrepreneurial mind, with an eye for growth and development.

Everything Giovanni has learned from school, from home brewing, and through Agostino's tutelage is put into practice. The results are immediate. Giovanni launches his first beer, Viæmilia, which becomes Del Ducato's flagship. A reflection of the Tipopils, the Viæmilia is dry hopped with Tettnang Tettnanger hops that Giovanni personally selects during the harvest. He's meticulous, comparing crops from different days and different fields.

In 2008, just one year after Del Ducato's opening, Giovanni's Verdi Imperial Stout is ranked first overall at the European Beer Star competition in Germany. It's the first Italian beer to ever win an international contest. The following year, the Nuova Mattina, a floral saison brewed with ginger, coriander, green pepper, and chamomile, is listed as one of the world's top twenty-five beers by *Draft* and *Wine Enthusiast* magazines.

The momentum picks up. In 2010, Viæmilia wins silver at the World Beer Cup and the Black Jack Verdi Imperial Stout takes two gold medals at the International Beer Challenge in London. More awards quickly follow. Only three years old, Del Ducato wins Italy's Brewery of the Year 2010 award and goes on to win four medals at the European Beer Star in Nuremberg, Germany. Giovanni doesn't rest on his laurels. In 2011, Del Ducato becomes the first Italian brewery awarded Brewery of the Year two years in a row. That same year at the European Beer Star, the Beersel Mattina, a lambic blend made in conjunction with Drie Fontainen Brewery in Belgium, and the Sally Brown win gold, accompanying seven other medals won by the brewery. Success and recognition continue in 2012 when the Viæmilia wins Silver at the World Beer Cup.

Del Ducato begins a climb to the top, cracking the ideologies of remaining small without compromising the artisanal concept. Like Teo, Giovanni and Manuel expand the idea of a larger artisanal picture: a fresh and balanced beer that is marketable where growth is not taboo.

"The domestic beer market is still young. In Italy, beer is the new frontier of taste, of drinking. Italian consumers are curious and willing, and very enthusiastic. The interest for craft beer is growing. There's a lot of potential here," says Giovanni.

Giovanni comes to represent the next generation of Italian craft brewers, enthusiastic creators who begin with home brewing kits and encompass everything that Agostino represents in his simple love of beer for beer's sake. He has the courage to become marketable without losing his soul. Giovanni is the sage like Agostino, and the trumpeter like Teo. He brews with a complete awareness of the process, devoted to excellence and never compromising quality—all this with

Danilo Troianiello, lead brewer for Del Ducato.

a goal for growth, not against it. With a strong business partner, Giovanni shines a light on the shadow cast by the bell tower and sheds *campanalismo* for a greater, national image of beer.

"Our brewing philosophy is to brew beers that, for how complex they can be, are always balanced and easily drinkable," explains Giovanni. "I have no brewing style, like I don't have a favorite meal. It's all about life and experiences."

Chapter 17
The Beer Freak Show

Bruno Carilli doesn't think *campanilismo*; he thinks *capitalismo*. Bruno Carilli is the owner and brewer for Toccalmatto, which means "a touch of madness." Perhaps it takes a dose of crazy to open a brewery in Italy, but Bruno brings something new to the table as Italian craft beer moves through its second wave, entering what is slowly becoming a viable market. Armed with an undergraduate degree in agricultural sciences and a master's degree in economics, Bruno is primed to push the wave forward. He has also gained experience in business as a manager of logistics for a few large international corporations, as in his seven years at Carlsberg, where they brewed 1.6 million hectoliters. As Bruno puts it, "They did more in spills than I do in pils."

Bruno finds his beer awakening while working in England. "I had the chance to taste some really, really interesting styles."

An opportunity at an English multinational corporation allows Bruno to indulge his interest in the English way of life. The first places he explores are the local pubs, where he discovers beer he can't find at home.

"The English beers I found in Italy were shit, really terrible—without sense, without taste. When I was in England, I had the chance to taste real ales."

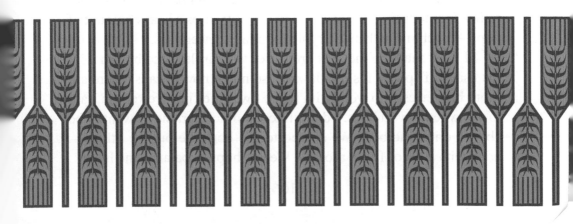

Upon his return to Italy, Bruno begins to brew at home, buying his first kit in 1992. Bruno is far ahead of his time. He's able to find hops and the equipment he needs from the United States through his connections to the international network.

"I've always had a big passion for hops, right from the beginning. My first beer, my preferred beer when I studied at Perugia, was Pilsner Urquell. It was better than it is now. It was so difficult at that time to find in Italy. But in Perugia, there was a small shop that had it."

In January of 1997, while working for Carlsberg in Milan, Bruno hears of the first Italian craft breweries opening in Italy. He immediately makes a pilgrimage to Birrificio Italiano, which is not even a year old. "For sure, I was influenced by Agostino. For me, Tipopils is a masterpiece."

Bruno transfers in 2005 to Fidenza, just a few miles up the road from Parma. Founded as a Roman camp named Fedentia, Fidenza became a *mucipium* of the Roman Empire in 41 BCE. Volleying through history from lordship to lordship, state to nation, Fidenza finally falls under one flag during the unification of Italy.

Bruno's experience as a big corporate manager pulls him from his roots in Umbria. Bruno's sense of *campanlismo* is rather watered down. For Bruno, Fidenza or Vicenza makes no difference. "I am not linked to the territory. Brewers like Riccardo at Montegioco are linked to their area and they want to remain small."

Once he locates to Fidenza, he meets fellow home brewers. Ready to take the step away from the international industrial world, he decides to start his own brewery in 2008, just a year after the nearby Birrificio Del Ducato.

Bruno's thinking is almost outside of the Italian, leaning more toward the American. Bruno is perhaps the first brewer in Italy who, rather than focusing on spices, sours, or nuts, uses a heavy amount of hops—much more than the typical Italian brewer uses.

"I think many of the first breweries were influenced by Teo with his usage of spices. It's not the case so much now because there are more breweries who work with hops. I was the first brewery in Italy to go extreme with hops. I don't like too much caramel. I want to be able to drink the beer. We started to use hops, before the others— hops with a lot of fruity aromas. We use hops to balance the hops."

Not one for sweet beer, Bruno has two lines: one more Belgian, the other more English and American, all characterized by dryness to enhance their drinkability.

"Our goal from the beginning was to only produce special beer, only beer with character. I wanted to remain an open-minded brewery, not too Italian. I am something more of an American, if you want. By more American, I mean I want to produce beer with more character."

Enjoying diversity, Bruno strives to use hops in innovative ways. "It's the best aspect of Italy: the diversity of food and wine and now beer."

Bruno decides to sell only to beer shops and to the best pubs in Italy. He sells a few to restaurants where the owners like beer, veering away from the normal pizzeria places or kebab shops. He develops a line especially made to be prepared with food "because a double IPA is very difficult to pair with Italian food."

The Italian beer drinker responds slowly to the hoppy beer Bruno produces. He sells practically nothing in his province of Parma. It's a slow evolution.

"It's different in the US, where breweries sell a lot in their local areas."

He sells bottles through his own shop mainly because there aren't many pubs in the province. There are some good places a couple of hours away in Milan, but the best market for Toccalmatto and the rest of Italian craft beer is found in Rome. Loaded with pubs, Rome is the engine that drives the movement, and Rome's consumers have discovered a love for IPAs. Toccalmatto finds its niche in Italy.

As more and more Italian craft brewers saturate the market in 2008, confusion arises in the consumers. "It's normal in a growing market. Every day there is a new brewery, so contamination happens through stupid beer, just someone making senseless beer like a light lager, a red or a brown."

This may sound familiar to the American craft-beer lover. In the mid-1990s, breweries such as Sierra Nevada, Anchor, and Bell's watched as the market around them became saturated with mediocre breweries that jumped on a bandwagon without giving a thought to what really mattered—great beer.

Today, the Italian craft-beer movement is facing a similar dilemma. Leaders such as Agostino, Teo, Lambrate, Campari, and Bruno are pushing the market along by continually innovating.

"I want to be pushing every day to do new things. The first point is quality and consistency. The second part is the ability to manage a business. You need to think towards the long term. Too many new breweries run their businesses on a day-to-day basis. Sometimes they make very good beer, but they can't run a business. I think there'll be a change like there was in the US. We haven't had that naturalization of the Italian market. In two or three years, the market will select the best."

Bruno Carilli, owner and brewer of Toccalmatto.

108

Part of Bruno's forward-thinking goal is to forge a more open environment. "Sometimes for the Italians and my colleagues, they have this culture of this legendary brewing figure, the man that must know all, the man that must do it himself, the legendary, mythological brewer: I have secrets. I am the god who wants to work on each brew myself, alone, because I am the owner—I don't agree with that. That's an American part of me. The Italian side of me is the inspiration and creativity. The Toccalmatto motto is to be open and innovative. I don't want to copy other beer. I'll be inspired, but not copy."

Bruno is the first in Italy to do collaboration brews. With Bruno's efforts, the closed atmosphere changes a little as he shares his experiences with others. "It's easier to work with foreign brewers because they are more open-minded to this kind of process. But now it's changing a little. After I did a few collaborations, some of the other breweries decided to do some of their own."

Bruno works with brewers as small as Montegioco, as off the radar as Spanish brewers, and as far away as Magic Rock in England. "I'm very proud to have a lot of brewery friends with whom I can debate and discover," he says.

Bruno consistently shuns *campanalismo* by virtue of his willingness to teach new brewers.

"I have three guys working for me, and each one of them must be able to make all the Toccalmatto beers. That way, I can continue to grow. It's more professional and American-style. Toccalmatto will work partially as a school, in this manner. There are some schools, but schools are one thing; brewing in a brewery is different. Giovanni Campari was a very good home brewer, but he took a paid training to work for Agostino where he really learned how to brew."

One of Bruno's former employees, Marcello Ceresa, is making a push on his own merits as the owner of Ritorto Brewery in nearby Piacenza.

"I told him, 'You must produce good beer.' I would've been upset if he didn't make good beer, because everyone knows he used to work for me. In fact, this year on Rate Beer, we got this certificate Best Brewer in Italy & Top 100 Brewers in the World, and the best new brewer is Marcello at Ritorto. I'm quite happy for Marcello. For me, it's good."

The Italian market is more or less a total of around seventeen million hectoliters of beer produced annually, with the microbreweries producing 100,000–150,000 hectoliters—that's about 80,000 barrels; it's nothing. But there is plenty of space for them to grow.

"At the beginning, there were the pioneers, not only as brewers, but also as publicans selling out of their pubs. And now we have to enlarge the market, selling off premises. During the first stage, not many of the microbreweries were making good beer. But now there's more confidence in the product. Obviously, not all breweries are making good beer. Out of the 500 breweries in Italy, only about twenty are able to produce good beer consistently. We have space to grow, and we have a lot of space abroad to grow, too.

"Toccalmatto is obliged to grow. We are currently brewing 1,400 hectoliters. I'm working on an investment plan to build a new brewery near the end of the year. The idea with the new brewery is to brew around 10,000 hectoliters. In Italy, 10,000 hectoliters is an ambitious goal. Today, it's Teo Musso and Del Borgo, both brewing 10,000 hectoliters and selling about half in their pubs."

Bruno is committed to this Italian experiment, and the great collaborator is set to expand on his ideas. "There's a phrase we wrote on the first page of our blog from Frank Zappa, one of my favorite musicians: 'The mind must be like a parachute; it is functioning only when it is open.' I love that phrase."

Chapter 18
Open Project

There are 300 breweries in Italy in 2008, accounting for 1 percent of the Italian beer market. Teo wonders why craft beer isn't being sold in bars and pubs. Perhaps because Baladin sells 92 percent of its beer in the wine world and many of the 300 breweries have followed him there.

"My project was born to sell to wine lovers. I'm doing a whole different thing by not selling to pubs. My goal isn't to sell my beer to beer people; it's to sell it to wine people to get closer to the wine world and to build more passion for beer. I designed my bottles to sit on the table of an Italian restaurant. I designed the Teku glass to bring in the flavor."

The Teku is the perfect beer glass to match the elegance of Teo's bottles on a fine dining table. The glass is shaped like the heart of an artichoke and closes at the top to soothe the aromatic needs of beer. In 2014, there will be 350,000 Teku glasses sold around the world.

While Bruno Carilli pitches his version of coexistence by way of collaboration, Teo has his own idea. He seizes on an open-source project born because, well, Teo does few collaborations. "In my opinion, it's one thing if it's a spontaneous idea and I just happen to be there and it's instinctive. Or, it must be a good, well-thought-out project that brings more to the table, because so many times, collaborations feel like marketing gimmicks."

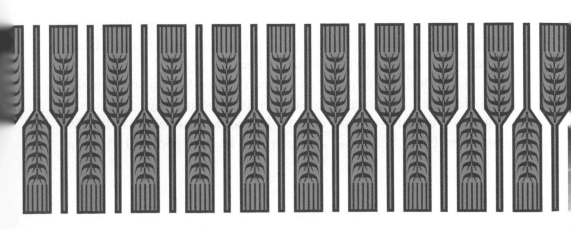

What Teo proposes is to redirect beer away from the wine table and out of the wine picture. His idea will be a mass shift and the birth of *the* Italian craft-beer market. In short, Teo will once again bring Italian craft beer into its own.

"Beer drinkers began to ask, 'Why can't I have Italian beer in my pub?' The project was designed to bring beer to a new market. Until 2009, 100 percent of Italian craft beer was sold in the wine world— all of it. There was no other branch for craft beer to be sold. But the problem was we were growing exponentially, and to give it sustainability, we needed to have a separate beer world. We were there to add a little color to the wine world, but eventually, thirty to forty million 750-millileter beers sold in wine bottles was going to piss the wine makers off. So let's open a new market. I wanted to redirect the market and bring the world of artisanal beer into the world of beer drinkers."

Like Bruno, Teo realizes he has to wrestle the Italian short-sighted hording of secrets. He does this by opening up completely. He launches the first open-source beer in history by publishing online one of his recipes for home brewers to compete over in a yearly competition. With exact instructions on how to brew his recipe on home brewing equipment, the challenge is to make its clone.

Teo has turned to the wellspring of all the newly generated brewers—the home brewers. He puts them up to a challenge: Brew my recipe, and whoever does it best will have their version brewed by Baladin and distributed to pubs and bars across Italy by the largest pub and bar distributor, Interbrau.

"I gave the keg distribution to Interbrau, the largest distributor of quality Italian beer, for three years."

Interbrau was started by Luigi Vecchiato shortly after World War II. Little by little, Luigi created a small distribution empire. Today, Interbrau is the distributor of quality beer in Italy.

"I did this Open Project as an open source for anyone to make it—Heineken, whoever. Published online, the message was, don't think about holding your secrets. It's better to coexist and grow together. Every year, I do an Open day. I spend about €100,000 a

year on research, and I put the data out there for everyone. We're all brewers; let's grow together."

Now that the Open Project has projected the Italian craft-beer world into pubs and bars, it's obvious to Teo what he has to do next—open *the* pub in Rome.

"In two years, I wanted this project to open a new arm of the market, because seeing a pub that was 100 percent Italian in the news and on television would show consumers that they could get Italian craft beer in a pub."

Rome is the target because it's the national news of Italy. La Republica is like the *New York Times*, and like Manhattan in the United States, Rome is the cultural heart of the nation. The idea is that if you can make it in New York, you can make it anywhere, so to make the news in Rome is to make yourself known to everybody. To do this, Teo's vehicle will be a bar unlike any other in Italy: one that will feature only Italian artisanal beers.

The instant you walk through the doors of Open Baladin, you know you're somewhere special. You can't help being overwhelmed by the jaw-dropping sight straight ahead. Hundreds of bottles stretch from the bar top to the ceiling, completely covering the fifty-foot-long wall. The bar, patrons, and taps are silhouetted by the bright lights shining on the statement that is Open Baladin's back wall. It says in an unmistakable, clear voice, "We have Italian craft beer." Playful art decorates the walls all around the bar, and a long chalkboard stretches across the side wall, displaying the available beers. The reaction is *wow!*

The effect of building a craft-beer market via Rome and Open Baladin is unquantifiable. Artisanal beer is now sold via forty taps in one location.

In the end, this could be Teo's greatest legacy, creating an Italian craft-brewing market where everyone is friends in the brewhouse and competitors only on the shelves, as it is in the United States. Open Baladin is a physical validation that Italian craft beer is worthy of its countrymen's notice and respect.

But the engine that drives all of this home is the forefather to Open Baladin, the Roman publican, and the conception of the Italian beer pub known as Macché.

Open Baladin, Rome.

Chapter 19
The Pillar of a Movement

"I was twenty-nine in 2001 when we opened Ma Che Siete Venuti a Fá. Rome was essentially excluded from what was happening in the north, where Italian craft beer was born. Here, nobody was making it. It didn't take off," says Colonna.

Ma Che Siete Venuti a Fá (informally known as Macché)—meaning "What the hell did you come here for?" an inference to the Roman smart-aleck attitude—is among the best pubs in Europe. Located in Trastevere, one of Rome's oldest boroughs, Macché opens originally as a soccer bar. Although the beer is always the main feature, Italian craft beer doesn't figure in immediately.

"Rome wasn't necessarily an ideal place to launch a revolutionary beer concept," Colonna explains. "Rome's never had a big interest in beer. We had a lot of Guinness pubs. In the 1980s and 1990s, we were invaded by Guinness. They turned so many places into tied houses that we had lost the independent pubs. It was Fabio Zaniol who pressed me. So when we decided to start a business together, I pushed this idea that publicans should own their own pubs."

In Italy, almost all pubs are connected to the distributor and are obligated to sell the distributor's beers. The term for these pubs is tied house because they are tied to their distributors or breweries. It's something that happens because Italy is still mainly selling industrial beers.

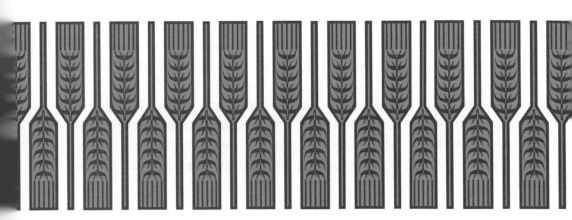

If Colonna had gone the tied-house route, he would've had two or three places and a Ferrari to boot. "But I would've failed because I wouldn't have had the product behind it."

Colonna realizes that only through independent pubs, with an owner who tastes the beer and learns how to maintain them, can his goal be achieved. Two fundamental people give Colonna the basis for Macché: Stefano Carlucci and Giorgione Chioffi. In Rome, these two men are considered the teachers for many publicans. Stefano owns one of the best whiskey bars in all of Europe, Le Bon Bock Café, located on the hills above Trastevere in the Monteverde area of Rome. Stefano has been around for twenty years, and while working at another pub, Colonna witnesses how Stefano travels to Germany and returns with German beer and, moreover, brings the tap system as well. It's a revelation to Colonna.

"I was just a drinker then, but when they poured beers, you could taste the difference."

Giorgione's famous pub Mastro Titta is the watering hole for many of the future Roman pub owners and brewers. Giorgione has been on the scene for years, and his influence on Colonna is unmistakable. Stefano gives Fabio and Colonna another view of the mechanics of a pub. Giorgione is the man who teaches the two men how to make money and the way to act around people, the little things about being a publican.

Fabio and Colonna find a small but workable location in the heart of Trastevere, one of Rome's most pristine boroughs, maintaining its characteristic cobblestone streets and medieval houses. Trastevere, like Greenwich Village in Manhattan, has always attracted unique characters, artists, expats, and celebrities. Its winding, narrow passageways are lined with pubs and restaurants. Several foreign academic institutions are located in Trastevere, many of which are of American or Canadian heritage. With the traffic of numerous students, tourists, and locals, Trastevere is an ideal and unique location for Colonna and Fabio's revolution.

Aiming to do something not found in Rome, Fabio and Colonna begin with a few unfiltered beers. They use a tap system that is adequate at the time for the style of beer they're serving, pouring beers with a nice thick head on top and in the correct glasses. They see the advantage of using the bar as a theater to showcase beer. They continue to widen the bar with more taps. Four become eight, and eight become twelve, until the taps reach the full length of the bar.

The tight quarters at Macché.

So small, this giant place, Macché, the bar is essentially a large master bedroom closet that could barely fit all of the brewing pioneers of 1996. On most nights, patrons spill into the street outside because there simply isn't room inside. Macché will come to define the Italian tap house. Aware of every detail, Colonna goes in search of the right people to work his pub. Every bartender has once worked at a well-known location and is handpicked by Colonna for professionalism and expertise in beer and bartending. "We began to meet well-known people who were very passionate. Paolo Pischi now works here, and Matteo Piergallini, too. Those guys were here from the first hour. Why aren't there brewpubs in Rome, but so many pubs and beer shops? Because everything was born in one pub and we all know each other. All of us. And there's a huge respect for one another."

For years, the beer movement remains in the area of the pioneers, the north, and doesn't move past that. Macché starts with a few European handcrafted beers on tap alongside a good selection of bottles. By 2003, everyone is referring to Macché in Rome, and sales multiply, but always, Colonna knows that Macché's advantage is its high standards. "You know, take care of it like you're supposed to. It's not that we're much better than other places; we just keep to our standards. It's easy. For me, the fundamental thing is a clean place, the right system, one that keeps the beer fresh. Like Americans who are really on it about using the right system, they know the difference in how to pour beer."

The true scope of the mission at Macché is to communicate a passion for beer, so Colonna begins to organize tastings. "Everybody's had a beer, but nobody knows anything about beer. If you can play this fact well and you're doing it honestly, then you have it. Then you can conquer a piece of the action."

Macché attracts a wide range of beer drinkers and draws—not just Italians, but an international beer crowd. It has come to be known as a place to enjoy and discover great beer, including Italian craft beer.

"I like it when you give a location a line of beers with reason. You could do a beautiful job with just six taps instead of fifty, if you offer six or seven well-thought-out taps, giving the client a path to follow in tasting, introducing various styles. Nobody made that step to communicate this beer movement to the people. Now people are asking, they know what they're interested in. It was really tough to get the Italian public to embrace craft beer."

The Italian craft-beer movement was thrown out to the masses. There's no mechanism that directs it, there's no association, something that can control the message. There are no directives, and there's no consistency. Freshmen craft drinkers go to one place and hear one thing, they go to another and hear another, and they don't know who's telling the truth. There's nowhere someone can go to become cultured in craft beer.

For this reason, in 2004 Colonna and Fabio open Bierkeller in the Testaccio borough. Bierkeller is like nothing else in the beer world— a members-only club for beer drinkers opens as a cultural club. The Bierkeller has a circle of beer enthusiasts that include some of the biggest names in the Italian beer world. Every month at the Bierkeller, a tasting is dedicated to one brewery.

"We did a tasting with Birrificio Troll, who had just opened, and Baladin. Teo brought a proto Xyauyú, his barrel-aged experiment. All the tastings were done by Kuaska. The place was beautiful, and it was big," recalls Manuele.

For people who won't go to Macché because of the compact chaos, Bierkeller is a place where they can get beer more comfortably. Colonna sets up a list of bottled beers that will allow him to explore taste sensations—sour, sweet, hoppy—and then bring them through a coursed meal. People who don't understand artisanal beer, common at this point in 2004, are thus given a chance to utilize Colonna's list of beers to open doors.

"It was a fantastic location where we could get people to understand what beer was."

Bierkeller is on its way to becoming the unofficial Italian cultural beer center. Then Bierkeller runs into its fate. Rome's a tough place to run a business, and because associations in Italy are nonprofit organizations with memberships, the proceeds are distributed to the daily running of the associations. There are many of these associations, and in many cases, they've gone out of control because it gives those looking to evade taxes an opening to not pay, so these types of clubs are constantly audited and regulated. It's not clear why, but Bierkeller becomes a target and is harassed weekly by checks and mandates, possibly because of a rival beer store in the neighborhood. In the end, a small discrepancy is enough to shut Bierkeller down.

The police director tells Colonna, "Cultural beer? You're trying to make fun of me. You're just here to circulate beer." Bierkeller was open for only a year.

Italy is always Italy, after all. "I hate to say it, but Italian laws always find a way to trample on you. Like when they made the laws about beer not being allowed off premises." A serious problem for a small pub like Macché.

"So we just became friends with the authorities. Obviously, there's not enough money to send the police everywhere. It's left in the hands of the pub owners, most of whom have more sensitivity to their wallets. We've made it for twelve years, so we must be okay— unless we get a new mayor who decides to shut us down."

The entrance of Macché with patrons spilling out into the street.

The key to what becomes Colonna's success isn't in the pub, or what beer he taps, but how he comes to know the brewers. And the person who gives Manuele the key to unlock this idea is Kuaska.

"When I met Kuaska in 2003, it was fundamental because I was introduced to great people like Andreas of Gaenstaller in Germany, Jean Van Roy of Cantillon, Kris De Dolle Herteleer in Belgium, and Dan Shelton. From these great people, I was able to learn and gain their knowledge of beer and work with them. I began to work with Dan Shelton importing craft beer from the US. This friendship allowed me to understand the brewers work. From this, I made the business decision to travel, choose beer, and import them as I got to know the brewers."

It's through these friendships that Colonna lays out the map for bringing beer in from all over Europe, keeping the Roman machine churning. It becomes an essential part of Manuele's business to know the brewers personally, going to their breweries to learn the personality of the brewer. Understanding a brewer is understanding what he brews. Like Birrificio Italiano with Agostino's knowledge of German beer, that's what Agostino does.

"When Giorgione from Mastro Titta and I went to visit Riccardo Franzosi at Montegioco, who is an incredible guy, who just is one of those people that takes you in, we found ourselves at a pub with him. He says, 'Let's try something.' At the end, we were left laughing and joking from noon until eight at night and there were twenty-seven empty bottles on the table. For Riccardo, it's that way and that's the point. In essence, you become part of a symphony. I don't know how else to explain it. Artisanal beer is now a business, but before, an artisanal brewer was doing it for passion, for fun. We come from that time."

Today, Rome is recognized as the hub for the Italian craft brewer, and since 2011, the scene has exploded.

It's not every year but every month that a new pub opens in Rome. Recently, five new locations opened just around Macché. It's become the fashion. There are now a hundred craft beer-focused pubs and sixty beer shops in Rome. Every area has its own beer shop.

Some places are insanely into beer. You breathe their passion. But they can become a bit obsessive. They're a bit like wine shops—snobby and a little aloof.

"Beer has to be fun. It should be the right element for a conversation between friends. Contrary to wine, beer is a fluid substance, it's everywhere. Beer is inclusive to all classes and cultures. It's not so much about business; it's a paradox," Colonna says.

As more and more pubs pop up, you increasingly run into pub owners who talk about beer like they know it but who have never visited a brewery. In a country where the personalities and territories are tied to the beer, this lack of connection to the brewer by the pub owner leads to a lack of understanding of the brewer's product.

"That care and sensitivity to each brewer and their beer isn't going to be met by every business owner now opening," says Colonna. But fundamentally, more locations opening leads to more people drinking beer, knowing about beer, and knowing the brewers.

"I consider these people great artists. Going to eat at their houses, opening up their first beers—these people came to my wedding. One of the brewers made a beer for my daughter. They have exceptional backgrounds. Visiting well-established breweries in history like Cantillon and opening up a bottle there, it feels like you're eating a family meal in the south of Italy, being in a small house, out in the garden. I have a huge respect for these things. The Italian brewers have a lot of respect for them.

"Even if I always believed in the potential of the movement, I had the fortune to have worked with what I like to do and the kind of people I like to be around. Even with Teo Musso with this enormous relationship, he's always exemplified this concept. As a man I appreciate him very much. Every time I see him, he takes me in like a brother. Even when he comes here, it's like a meeting of friends."

This small, tightknit group of friends are who open the initial locations for beer in Rome. "We'd go out together and have parties together. Mastro Titta, Il Serpente, Il Birrifugio Ostia, Stefano Frasca, a very good publican, and even Alex Liberati at Brasserie 4:20.

"The legend wants to say Alex and I were never friends. He's got a particular character. He's always been one of our clients, even since he was seventeen. Philosophically, we were very different, but Brasserie 4:20 is one of those places the whole movement exploded from, without a shadow of a doubt."

Chapter 20
The Punk-lican

"At the time, there weren't a lot of beer bars in Rome—just me and Manuele—and there was a lot of fighting going on, which didn't help the Roman beer culture at all. We didn't get along very well when we were younger. I was one of his clients when he was still serving industrial beer, and I was drinking it, so it goes back to before the start of everything."

Alex Liberati isn't your typical Roman. His mother's English, from Hartfordshire, and his father is from Rome. Raised in Rome, this very intelligent young man has a restless soul and a fierce, independent streak. Regardless of where Alex might have been raised, he would have always been the outsider, the rebel. It's just in his nature. The Italian craft-beer world is a place made for such a young man, and he takes to it with the passion of the newly converted.

Never one to like wine, the twenty-year-old Alex is an early beer drinker, by chance. Alex spends his time hanging out at a late-hours bar where he plays chess until six a.m. With limited choices, Alex drinks a 9 percent industrial beer called Super Tennants while playing. By three o'clock in the morning, Alex is too drunk to play chess. He realizes he'll never get his game together if he continues drinking 9 percent beer, so he looks for an easier beer to drink. He discovers a 5 percent beer called Young's Pale Ale. He's surprised at the difference in taste. He takes an

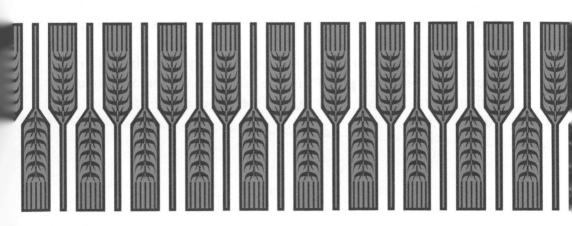

immediate liking to the beer and wants more. Naïve, Alex goes in search of the source, but in the wrong place.

To Alex, all beer is made in Germany, so he treks to Germany, not knowing Young's is actually English. In Germany, he discovers a new beer world and realizes he can't find any of the beer he's getting on his trips to Germany in Rome, so he brings back some of the beer he likes in his Volkswagen station wagon. Able to fit twenty-two crates in his Volkswagen, he travels back and forth. The customs officers, more concerned about people bringing back marijuana, laugh at him every time he crosses the border. When his friends try Alex's beers, they become enthusiastic.

"I could see there was something behind it. I could see they were liking it."

On one of Alex's trips, a man he meets is shocked to learn that Alex has never been to Belgium.

"What? Belgium does beer? So I started going to Belgium. Wow, discovery. De Dolle. Drie Fontainen. All the great stuff. I was just a kid going around knocking on brewery doors. I had this book and actually met the guy who wrote the book in a café in Belgium."

Alex begins regular excursions, driving between Belgium and Rome once a month, bringing twenty-two crates of beer back with him and having parties with his friends.

"I was in school, so I had a lot of free time during the day. Eventually, I decided to drop it all and open a bar."

The problem is, his mother wants Alex to be a violinist and his dad wants him to be an architect or doctor. "You can imagine the fright when I told them, 'I'm going to drop school, get out of the house'—because I was still living with them at the time, as all Italians do—'I'm going to start my own thing. I don't care what it's going to take.' They thought about it and said, 'Well, okay, we'll give you a hand.'"

It takes Alex a year to find a place and two years to build it. He opens his seventy-tap pub, Brasserie 4:20 near the famous Roman market, Porta Portese, close to the Tiber River at the beginning of 2007.

Brasserie 4:20 taps.

"I was very keen to get the beer I was loving from Belgium and Germany."

The most immediate problem Alex faces are distributors in Rome. "It gets up to 100 °F in Rome in the summer. You can't keep beer in a hot warehouse. The beer's going to destroy itself. Even the strongest beers I drank at the time from Belgium were so different from what I got when I was there."

Frustrated, Alex, who is like the blue-collar Teo Musso, finds a solution: He'll just import his own. "I bought a van. I started going up and down from Holland and Belgium, and I met some people who had warehouses and filled my van with interesting stuff."

Alex launches his import company Impex in 2008, storing empties on his roof and moving everything by hand.

"It was insane. That summer, I remember, we kept empty kegs on this rooftop. We had to send like 200–300 kegs back to the suppliers in August on a hot day, the sun was vertical, and we had to lower these kegs from the roof by hand with a rope two or three at a time.

That was one of the worst days of my life. We did that for a while. Finally, I bought a warehouse with a forklift."

Alex is the first to bring American beers to Italy. "We had Titan IPA from Great Divide in Denver, Colorado, which was one of the breakthroughs here. Unfortunately, they're not selling here anymore because of fears of oxidation. I had brought beer to the Great British Beer Festival in England, and on the way down, I stopped at a distributor in Belgium who I knew. He had called me and said, 'Come on by, I've got some killer stuff.' So I did and filled my van with stuff like Titan IPA and Hercules Double IPA from Great Divide. I got it two months before anyone else in Italy did. We had a line out the door two blocks long. It was amazing. People were loving the hops. There are people who work for me who started drinking hops that night, and we reminisce about that time. It was a really cool thing."

Always pushing the envelope, Alex strives to find the unattainable to present to his customers. Not many people in Europe, and especially Italy, are familiar with American-style barleywines.

"They have no idea it's hoppy. If you look at the style charts, you'll see it's at the very top of the hop range. Everyone here only knows the English barleywines, so a lot of people who taste this beer say, 'No it's not a barleywine.' It's an American barelywine, not an English one."

Alex has always made it a point to be the pinnacle for hoppy beers. He's not the father of hops in Italy—that title goes to a predecessor, Mike Murphy—but Alex is certainly an anchor and a resource for the ever-growing hop palate of Romans.

"We did a Colorado beer festival here with Doug Odell from Odell Brewing along with Left Hand Brewing. We refrigerated the beer all the way from Colorado. It was expensive, but all the beer bars in Rome got some and it was cool. People were drinking fresh, great hoppy beer. In December, we flew in a pallet of the freshest, made-yesterday IPAs from Pizza Port in San Diego, California. So it was like being there. Twelve of them came over. It was amazing. We had a great night. Manuele was in tears."

Always the anarchist, Alex pushes the boundaries in all categories. "We were the first to use a jar in Italy. People went wild. Some loved it, some hated it. One of the reasons we started to use the

The Punk-lican, Alex Liberati.

Mason jar was because there are a lot of people who need to drink the right beer in the right glass or get totally picky about the temperature it's served. It's a big pain in the ass. How many times do you get some people sitting at the bar and they make the game of Find the Mistake? One suggests to the next that there's .01 percent diacetyl in the beer, and the next believes it. We get a lot of this happening now. It's beer. Okay, it's got a touch of diacetyl. Drink another beer!

"It's getting to be too much. Hopefully, in the next five years, people will get more laid back about it. We have a lot of rules, rigidity with the right glass and the right temperature. We have people that make a riot out of it if we don't have the right glass. People freak out about our pitchers. Who cares? It's good beer. Just drink it. We have a video of this glass breaking a Teku. I don't give a shit, we're talking about craft beer. This jar has a history behind it, the Mason jar. It's pretty close to craft brewing. It has a reason. Some people probably like it because of that. This jar is everywhere in the US.

"It became our way to tell people to get more laid back about beer. Drink from the bottle. Drink from the jar, just enjoy it. We have our own growlers, and we were the first to do them here. People said we were silly when we started, but now even beer shops are doing it.

In 2011, Alex opens a company in San Diego called Noble Beverages to export American beer to Italy. He receives his license, finally, in the summer of 2012.

"Brewers in Italy want to export because they think it's going to be so great, but you're selling to just one customer. What if he closes your tap? Well then, now you have all this big extension with no one to sell to. Also, you're working for nothing. To get beer to Australia, you have to put a markup so slight, because everyone needs to make money along the way. This is a recipe for disaster. You're building a very fragile business to be able to sell to not a lot of people who can crush you when they want. And everyone in Italy is trying to export. What they don't realize is they should concentrate on Italy.

"As a brewer, I made the same mistake with my Revelation Cat beers. It was all about the love of seeing my beer in Japan. I went to this Japanese beer festival and they had our beer, and I loved it. It was really cool. It was extremely satisfying for my ego, that's it. But, no, you need to build a steady business with the guy down on the corner. You've gotta love him, and he's gotta love you. You've gotta sell beer in a passionate way. You've gotta do that, but they just don't get it.

"I like the idea that there's gonna be craft beer around. I remember when I started out, it was terrible. There was no craft beer anywhere. You couldn't go drink anywhere; you had to drink at home. This last year's been great and especially here in the Lazio region."

In 2009, there is a lot of fighting between Manuele and Alex, a rivalry, but Brasserie 4:20 has been important to the Roman scene, the Italian scene, because Alex is bringing beer from all over the world—imperial stouts, hoppy American beer, extreme stuff. That initial tension and animosity between the two men gives way to cooperation and respect. After going to his first Craft Brewer's Conference in the United States, Alex comes to a realization. "They kept repeating to me 'An incoming tide lifts all boats.' I came back and spread this here. Luckily, it's now all changed between Manuele and me. We've grown up. He's got a kid. I've grown up. There is, of course, some competition, but it's for the good. It's a bigger picture. There are six million people in Rome, with 5,500 bars and restaurants, and there's only about fifty that serve craft beer. There's room for everybody. But the younger publicans, they're so fearful. They just don't get it now. I didn't in my time. Manuele didn't in his time. We do now. They don't get it now, but they will in the future."

Chapter 21
An American Rebel in Rome

Before Manuele opened Macché and long before anyone else had opened a brewery in Rome, a Philadelphian wove relationships that are at the heart of today's Roman craft-beer scene and set a precedent that opened doors for every brewer in Italy who followed.

In 1999, Mike Murphy is a twenty-seven-year-old student at Rome's Temple University campus, studying landscape architecture. While in Rome, he falls in love with a woman who owns a bar called Starbess, just north of the Vatican. Mike is about to make history in a city chock full of it.

In 2000, there isn't a high hope in hell of finding a good, hoppy American beer. Mike knows the answer lies in making it himself. On Mike's nineteenth birthday, his father gave him a home brewing kit and as the American craft-beer movement gained momentum in the 1990s, Mike followed closely, "with my glass."

As for any skilled home brewer, the short step to becoming a professional brewer is too tempting for Mike to pass. He tries to convince his Italian girlfriend that they should convert her pub into a brewpub. She's not easily persuaded, as most Italians during this period would not be. Nevertheless, Mike's ambitions grant him a space a few meters from the pub, and Mike sets out to quench his thirst. He begins brewing on a small scale but quickly catches the

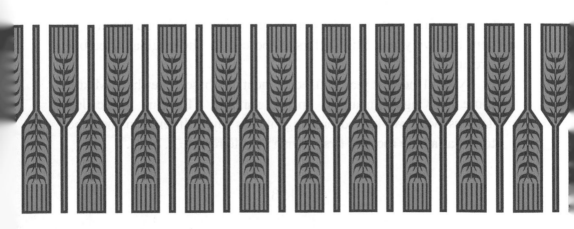

attention of the very few swimming the Italian suds, including Kuaska and Manuele Colonna.

It's not long before Mike's attention turns toward a more ambitious idea—to create a 5,000-hectoliter brewpub in urban Rome. To do such a thing in Turin is still as unimaginable as reaching the moon by civilian transport, but to open a brewpub in Rome is like colonizing Mars.

Although there was actually one brewery in Rome before Mike's in the late 1990s, the effect Mike will have on Italian craft beer grants him an honorary first place. His predecessor was called Brew People and was located in Piazza Cavour.

"They did it all wrong. They bought their system through Criveller, who has a sister company in northern Italy who are brewing equipment manufacturers. They sell you this song and dance that they'll train your brewer in two weeks when you buy their system. So they did that, and one of the owner's sons was trained, but he didn't know what he was doing. You can't learn to brew in two weeks, especially a nineteen-year-old who's never done anything in his life. He said the beer was so bad that they'd pour a beer and by the time it got to the table, half the glass was yeast."

Brew People shut down within six months.

While looking for brewing equipment and thinking about his concept, Mike has a lot of free time on his hands. A little homesick, Mike frequents an American-style bowling alley nearly every day. On one occasion, he pops his head around the back and finds an entire seven-barrel brewhouse with tanks under a tarp. Mike discovers that the owner of the bowling alley is one of the owners of Brew People.

Mike tries to buy the equipment, but the owner won't budge on the price. He wants what he paid new for it, but he's had the equipment for five years. Mike offers 30 percent of the original price but is refused.

By April the next year, with equipment purchased elsewhere, Mike's Rome Brewing Company is up and running. "The pub was called Starbess when we started brewing; it was my girlfriend's name. The story was a little rocky at first. I wish I could rewrite it, but…"

Mike has set Starbess on a trajectory to reach the stars. He's got the equipment to build a 5,000-hectoliter-per-year brewery, but no place to do it in, and strapped for cash, he has no money to buy a space. But Mike's beers are already building him a fan base. Like moths to a light, young, innovative thinkers with a healthy curiosity and interest in what Mike is doing are gathering at Starbess.

Mike's Pioneer Pale Ale is a palate shocker to any Italian, but home brewers and anyone with a penchant for something foreign, something innovative, make a pilgrimage to Starbess to meet this rebel American brewer. It's the only place where Italian brewers can go to have American-inspired beers from someone whose brewing origins are based in the American craft-beer movement. It's a testament to how far ahead Mike and the American scene are. Italy's brewing movement is still in its infancy, but Mike quickly gains high status.

"I'm not the one who invented the American pale ale. I just did what I do, what I like, and I just did it there. Any American brewer in my situation would've done the same. It just happened to be me."

Mike doesn't hold back. He brews beer that even for the American craft-beer scene would be regarded renegade. Mike brews a barely wine, called the Maelstrom, with an alcohol content of 16 percent, along with a strong ale clocking in at 12 percent. For the common Italian who might stroll into Starbess and find himself in front of six taps with homemade beer, the concept of what Mike is doing is far beyond their comprehension.

"It was a lot of explaining. I had to do a lot of one-on-one educating. It felt like I was wasting my breath on 99 percent of the people. You give a long introduction on most people, and you want them to know what they're getting into and you almost want to tell them, 'Don't try it. You're not gonna like it.'"

One young, fervent home brewer loves what Mike is dishing out and gobbles it up nearly every night. The young biochemistry PhD student, Leonardo Di Vincenzo, and Mike quickly become friends.

"I met Leonardo when I first came to Italy. I was getting ready to order some small brewing equipment from this guy who built little breweries from way up north. Leonardo was an avid home brewer, and the guy who sold me the equipment brought Leonardo in case I needed some help or something. I think Leonardo understood right away that I'd be fine without him. But we shared a common interest. It was rare in Rome at that time. There weren't a lot of people that had that common interest. I think it was just me and him."

"I started home brewing in 1996–1997," says Leonardo, "just to save money instead of going to pubs on weekends. I said to my friends, 'Let's home-brew and save money.' In the end, I spent much more than if I had just frequented the pubs. In 2002, I started my PhD, and in 2003, I became good friends with Mike. Mike had a really small place in Rome called Rome Brewing Company, selling his beers from a small pub called Starbess."

Mike and Leonardo begin to take trips together, traveling Europe, studying and drinking beer from the gems of the beer world: London, Germany, and, of course, Belgium.

But others are also stopping by Starbess—early names from the dawn of Italian craft beer, like Agostino Arioli from Birrificio Italiano. Another man who would seem an unlikely candidate for the future beer scene lumbers into Starbess—a pizza maker named Gabriele Bonci.

"One day this guy, a big, intimidating dude with a similar personality to mine—loud, boisterous, and kind of sloppy; we're both big and bald—times two, walks in. He came in the bar, and I'm standing there behind the taps with my girlfriend right next to me. He walked in and announced that he loves fermentation. Already, I thought he was a little strange, but I liked him. For some reason, I liked him. It's not often an Italian guy comes in the door and tells me 'I love fermentation.'

"He tried every single one of my beers. I had six beers on tap, and he drank a pint of each in about ten and a half minutes. One after another, he drank them down to the bottom, looked at me, and said, 'Buona.' He went right through them all. And my girlfriend's thinking, 'Is he going to try and turn and walk out of here without paying?' She started getting nervous. Anyway, he paid his money and walked out.

"The next day he showed up and did it all over again. He told me he owned a pizzeria called Pizzarium. He said he did something special with the pizza, and I'm like, hmmm, interesting. But I was pretty busy and didn't think much about it. He gave me his card. I think a couple of days went by and I was working and getting hungry and thought, 'I have a little time, maybe I should go down and check this guy out.' I went down there, and there was a bunch of people that seemed like they just lived inside this tiny pizza shop, like they just stayed there all day long. Gabrielle was very happy to see me there and never let me one time pay for pizza. Even if I went there today, they'd probably recognize me and tell me, 'You don't pay.'"

"I met Bonci when I was working at Starbess," recalls Leonardo, "because his pizzeria was close by. And before I started working at Starbess, I would go to his pizzeria for pizza. Bonci had just opened, and he was so sad because he wasn't having any success. He complained, 'No one likes my pizza, but I think it's good pizza.' We became friends. He would come over to Starbess and drink beer, exchanging ideas."

Together, Teo Musso(left), Chef Gabriele Bonci(center) and Leonardo Di Vincenzo(right) will collectively open Bir e Fud, Open Baladin, NO.AU in Rome creating a buzz throughout the beer world.

"The pizza blew my mind, it was so good," says Mike. "I just ended up being very active with Bonci, and I knew he liked beer, so I started taking him out to the best beer bars in town at the time—places like Sensa Fondo and Manuele's Macché and his other project going at the time called Bierkeller."

"Consider that in 2002–2003, the beer world in Italy was really tiny," remembers Leonardo, "so everybody in the beer world was involved with each other. We were friends and helped each other. When Manuele opened Bierkeller, I was helping him choose beers, setting up tastings and cultural events. I was just a home brewer, but I had become a taster for Slow Foods and a teacher for Slow Food courses. This was my side job, helping me to gain knowledge in the beer world. When Manuele opened Bierkeller, we decided to have a selection of Italian breweries, and I was just starting to do these kinds of small events, and so we had become close friends."

"I had to do a beer tasting there, and Leonardo did the talking because I felt like he would do it better than me," says Mike. "I asked Gabriele if he would like to bring some of his pizza to try with my beer. He brought a lot of pizza, and there was room for about fifty people, and he ended up talking about his pizza."

Known in Rome as Il Giocolo della Pizza, which means "the pizza juggler," Bonci was baptized "the Michelangelo of pizza" by *Vogue* magazine. Bonci's 200-year-old mother yeast, along with his inventive and innovative toppings, will come into play with nearly every pioneer in the Italian craft-beer scene in Rome. In essence, Bonci renews pizza and beer, taking it from its old, dismissive industrial pairing to the current artisanal one, but in 2003, Bonci is an unknown guy with a little pizza shop around the corner from Starbess.

Right around this time, Mike's plans begin to come unraveled.

"It all started when I broke up with that girl. We started getting serious about the brewery, and that's why we broke up. We weren't really a great couple anymore, but we decided to be serious and go forward with our plan."

Mike is sustaining himself in Rome. He's broke, but he has his equipment stockpiled, waiting to build a significantly sized microbrewery for Italy. He finds a few people interested in his idea, but every time he hits a roadblock, they give up. Perhaps it is just a little too soon, or maybe he just didn't find the right people. Regardless, Mike's ambitious idea is slipping away.

"Italian people are hard to deal with sometimes in business, and that was a lot of money. I was looking at a 5,000-hectoliter brewery.

That was my goal. It would've been a whole different story for my life. I'm sure I would've been rockin' and rollin' right now."

The final plunge of the dagger for Mike is when his girlfriend meets another man. The couple marries six months later.

"He threw a monkey wrench in the works because he didn't want me around. He made it very difficult for me to do this business with my ex-girlfriend, and he tried to get involved and act like my boss. Also, above my little brewery, some people moved in and they had good connections and they didn't like me down there, so they had the police show up and fine me for every little thing. After a few months of getting those fines, I said to them, 'If I promise to close down by the end of the year, will you stop having me fined?' So they stopped and I closed by the end of the year."

"In 2003, I was helping Mike," Leonardo says. "He wanted to return to the US on vacation. I spent a month brewing with him. After he went on vacation, his girlfriend broke up with him. He remained outside for six months, so I brewed there for six months. When he came back, I left the brewery and returned to the university, but by then, I was thinking about opening my own brewery."

About 2004, Mike moves to Perugia in central Italy, east of Tuscany, with people running a brewery called La Sera.

"They had a nice little brewhouse and they had some money. During that time, people were thinking this was a lucrative business. You meet these kinds of people along the way. They too were misguided by the equipment salesman, who was just trying to make some money, so they didn't know how to brew and I did, so I made a deal with them: 'If you let me brew my beer there, I'll pay for the ingredients for my own brews. I'll brew four batches a month for your restaurant. And I'll also train your eighteen-year-old nephew how to brew.' I did that for about six months. I was making beer for my Rome Brewing Company, and I was actually selling it better than when I had my own little brewery. I had more free time, and I was making more money than I was used to having."

Eventually, Mike finds himself in need of a different situation. His brewing equipment provides him with a ticket out. "I looked at three or four different places and talked to some different people, but it requires a lot of money for a space, to renovate and get it set up.

The cost of the equipment isn't even half the expense. I thought it was the main expense. I had about $190,000 wrapped up in it. It was all loans, and I had to pay that off. So I just put it up for sale to get out of it."

A Danish company looking to start a brewery buys Mike's equipment and asks if he will come along and help them for a few months with the initial start-up. Mike jumps at the offer. It pays well, and it's a good way for Mike to get out from under the loan. "But I also always wanted to try brewing on that equipment," says Mike. "I had been looking at it laying on its side on a pallet and thinking, 'I want to brew on this thing.' So I was eager to do that."

While he's waiting for the Danish deal to come together, Mike reaches out to his old friend Leonardo. Leonardo has been busy working on opening a brewery in a small town seventy kilometers northeast of Rome. Mike helps Leonardo put tiles up at the brewery as Leonardo finishes two of what will become Del Borgo's flagship beers, the ReAle and the ReAle Extra, recipes based on Mike's ideas. These two beers will soon become a major hit.

Mike can feel the changes around him and also in his friend, Leonardo, a little weirdness between them. "He was still kind of small at the time, but he's gotten big with a new brewery and got in with the right people."

"The ReAle Extra from Leonardo comes out in 2005 or 2006," Manuele says. "It was the era of the IPAs. They're easy to drink, and they shock the Italian palate to God. It's the most valid thing you can have on the market. It began a disaster in Rome with everyone following it—a chain reaction."

It is because of Mike Murphy that in the near future, Brew Fist and Toccalmatto will find a willing audience for their strong, hoppy beer.

Mike's month in Denmark turns into three years, until the brewery is sold, but people in Rome are still talking about Mike's beer. Mike returns to Italy in 2008 with the intention of staying permanently. His old friend Leonardo gives him a job at the fledgling brewery Birra Del Borgo, but Mike's in love once again, with a woman in Denmark, and decides he can't stay in Italy.

"I went to Italy in 2008 to live and work with Leonardo. Right away, I felt I wanted to go back. Right away, I felt a huge difference in how free I felt in Denmark compared to Italy. Denmark's much more relaxed than Italy is, and I started realizing that. I always felt very free in Italy when I was younger 'cause I wasn't taking things seriously.

"I felt bad because I kinda felt like I screwed Leonardo over. I think that damaged our relationship a little bit, by not staying to work with him. I think it's good we had our own path—something together as equals, not me working for him. He surpassed that, and I couldn't come in as an equal at that point with him."

Mike Murphy has been at the right place at the right time, but perhaps not with the right people. Today, he is regarded as one of the most influential brewers in the second wave of Italian brewers. His hoppy beers forever change the horizon of the Italian craft-beer movement. No doubt, Mike Murphy has left a mark on the scene, and that's good, but unfortunately, that doesn't pay the bills.

After returning to his girlfriend in Denmark, Mike is given an opportunity to brew at Lervig Brewery on the north coast of Norway in the town of Stavanger. "I didn't want to leave Denmark, but I couldn't find anything, and this opportunity seemed pretty good," says Mike.

Even though Mike is in Norway, Manuele Colonna keeps his name circulating.

"I didn't go to Italy much at all this year, but I went down there seven times last year," says Mike. "I even brewed a commemorative batch of Pioneer Pale Ale with Leonardo, and we sold it for a few months down there.

"I made a lot of beer in Denmark and hardly made a dent. People know me and I'm remembered in Denmark, but not like I am in Italy. In Italy, they treat me like a rock star."

Chapter 22
Catching the Wave

While Mike Murphy finds happiness and a home in Norway,
Leonardo Di Vincenzo is just getting cranking. Leonardo heralds the
third generation. The Italian craft-beer world remains turbulent, but
one thing is certain: Italy will never be without craft beer. There's no
going back. Even if every brewery shut down today, a generation of
Italians brought up on craft beer would seek to make their suds in
their way in some fashion tomorrow.

Leonardo, like many of his generation of brewers, has home-
brewed his way to an apprenticeship and then onto his own brewery,
but Leonardo finds himself in a unique position—he is a brewer
from Rome. He's been in the most innovative beer pubs, worked and
made strong friendships with the publicans and brewers. His friendship with Mike Murphy teaches him how to navigate the tempestu-
ous seas of owning a brewery, while Manuele Colonna teaches him
about being a publican, a brewery's life source. Well-connected and
well-versed in his field from food to wort to pub, Leonardo is suffi-
ciently armed to lead the movement to its next level.

Birra Del Borgo is born in 2005 in the small village of Borgorose, an hour's drive northeast of Rome and surrounded by the
snowcapped Apennine Mountains at the border between Lazio and
Abruzzo. Del Borgo starts off as a tiny little building about the size

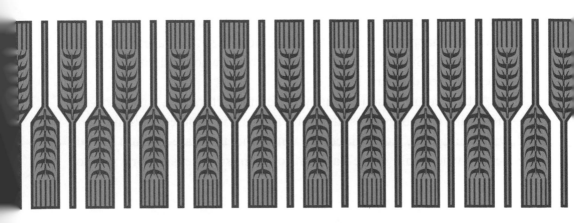

of a private mechanic shop, where not all the vats and boilers fit and things have to be constantly shifted around. "It was like playing Tetris, moving tanks around," Leonardo recalls. It's here where some of Del Borgo's most famous recipes are created: ReAle, Duchessa, and DucAle.

The old Del Borgo brewery now fitted with a koolschip where they will make spontaneously fermented beer.

"When we started, it was hard to sell a bottle of ReAle because it was considered too hoppy," says Leonardo. "Craft beer was coming to Rome, but it was mainly beer like Baladin, Belgian-style beer, sweet beer, very fruity, very high in alcohol. But there was a small revolution happening within the movement in small places in Rome, like Ma Che Siete Venuti a Fá and Starbess, who brought people to a new idea of drinking beer."

"It's a combination of many different factors that gave birth to the Italian craft breweries; the same is true with Rome," says the beer writer and judge Luca Giaccone. "In Rome, there are lots and lots of people who drink. There's a lot of tourism, so it's easier for a pub to be busy all day and all week. In Rome, you can open at five p.m. and sell beer. In Turin, no. In Turin, you have to wait for people to go home, eat dinner, and then they go out for the night. I think the most important point is the huge curiosity of Romans. They want to discover. When you go to Macché and you listen to the people coming in, the first thing they say is, 'What's new?' In my town in the Piedmont, it's the opposite. If a pub has five beers on tap and they change one, some guy will come in and ask, 'Where's my beer? What can I drink now? My beer's gone.'"

"I can say we—Italian craft brewers—are lucky because we only had industrial beer before we arrived," Leonardo says. "But we have a long gastronomical history and huge gastronomical influences. About twenty years ago, Slow Food was born in Italy. They tried to preserve the old, traditional food, the old way of making food. When I was young, my mother was very traditional and grew up in this area buying the local cheeses and breads and such. But in the 1980s, this idea grew that you should stay away from those kinds of foods because they weren't safe and you should eat sterilized foods. Slow Food was born to save those foods; it's just the opposite. You need that traditional stuff. It's the difference, it's the variety, the complexity. It is so close to what's happened to beer because the brewers agree, we don't need to focus on styles. We can do whatever we want. That's the future."

"It's not by choice that in 1996, the Salone Del Gusto was held for the first time and the first craft brewery was born," says Luca Giaccone. "It's something that runs on a parallel path. The originality of taste in Italy is very important. Every single region in Italy has its own food, its own taste, so beer has to be different in every region. In Lazio, they love hops, to say the first thing that comes to mind. In Piedmont, they love more alcohol in their beer. Every region has a taste."

"I think the most important thing is we don't have rules in brewing, but we have taste," explains Marco Pion, co-owner of BiDu Brewery near the Swiss border, north of Milan. "So on the other side of things, the Germans have rules, but they don't have taste, so they go on doing the same thing. When they do it well, it's fabulous, but they will not put something more in it. Italians have two things: They have taste, so they know that this wine or beer will pair well with this food, and the second thing is Italians are good at mixing things up. They can mix up a recipe and turn out a dish. We have brewers who have an idea of what they want to brew, and it's often something that's not present on the market. Why would you brew a clone of Del Borgo's ReAle? We will do something unique. We know where we want to go, and we're learning how to reach our goals. It's not all gold. There are something like 500 breweries in Italy, and probably half of them don't have the slightest idea of what they are doing. It's not a game where you can open a brewery and it will pay your bills. It's just not true."

With Del Borgo's kickoff in 2005, there's immediate praise around the beer world, but commercially speaking, it's not so easy. Del Borgo struggles for the first two years. Part of Del Borgo's future success is having Rome close by with a beer drinking audience ready to try something new. But Del Borgo really accelerates when Manuele Colonna and Leonardo Di Vincenzo decide to take a big chance.

"Our idea was to only feature Italian beer at a restaurant so that the Italian people would see that it was possible to just work with Italian beer," explains Leonardo. "The Italian craft-beer market at that time wasn't so easy because there were some breweries selling all over Italy, but craft beer was in the wine world. It was easier to sell craft beer in wine bars, like Teo Musso's Baladin beer. But it was the only way to sell beer at that time. We were selling Italian beer, but in small quantities, and people didn't trust Italian craft beer because it was inconsistent, with no stability behind the beer, so there wasn't much confidence to sell Italian craft beer.

"The beer and food connection was always so important, and still today, all Italian craft beer relies on a small sell of food. Most beer in Italy is sold to be paired with food, and this is really an important part of Italian beer." There is no one willing to risk opening a beer bar like Manuele and Leonardo are thinking.

No one has thought to bring a full beer list with all Italian beer from all the best craft breweries into a restaurant setting. It's a risky idea in 2007. So far, brewers are able to sell to local restaurants, but mainly as a wine substitute, or they open a brewpub and sell their own beer in a pub setting. Places like Grato Plato in Chieri take this concept to the highest level. Macché showcases Italian craft beer, but there's no food. Manuele and Leonardo's idea is an original concept for Italy, but how people will react to it is a tough calculation. Italians, even in Rome, don't believe in the credibility of beer, especially Italian-made beer. The concept to create a business against the culture doesn't exist in Italy. For an American, against-the-grain is a way of life, a means to success, originality, counterculture, but messing with Italians' deeply embedded ideas of food is truly risky, especially when you're banking on pairing Italian beer with food.

Leonardo is convinced this will work. His back is up against the wall; business at the brewery isn't going so well. But Manuele isn't as convinced. It takes Leonardo a little time to win him over. "I kept telling him, we *need* to do this."

In an attempt to push themselves out of the wine world, Leonardo and Manuele decide to go back to an old tried and true concept: beer and pizza, with a twist.

A throwback to the old beer-and-pizza combination, Bir e Fud is not your typical pizza joint. For one, the pizzas are by their old friend, Gabriele Bonci, and the beers are far from cold, dead industrial lagers. "We wanted to prove that the pizza-and-beer pairing, a classic in Italy, could find a new meaning by matching craft beer with gourmet pizzas and other simple but well-prepared dishes," Manuele says.

Bir e Fud opens with twelve beers on draft. Three or four taps are reserved for Del Borgo; the rest are from other Italian breweries: Troll, Baladin, Birrificio Italiano, Del Ducato, Extraomnes, Almond 22, and more.

"I remember the first kegs we sold were always tricky stabilizing the beer. We were working directly with the breweries because there was no distribution," Manuele says.

Bonci in 2007 is a well-respected and up-and-coming star, but people are baffled—indignant, even—that Bonci's high-end food is being paired with beer. The critics insist that Bonci's food must be paired with wine. Letting Bonci's food speak for itself, Manuele and Leonardo just focus on the beer. They spend every night for four months explaining each beer, giving small samples, and doing tastings. For Leonardo, this period is a tough time. He's brewing beer during the day an hour away in Borgorose and retuning to Rome each night, working the pub. It pays off. People are not talking about Bonci's food alone; they're talking a lot about the beer.

Six months from the opening of Bir e Fud, the beer market really explodes. Italians, even if still a small proportion, are finally realizing they can work with Italian beer. Manuele jumps at the opportunity and begins to collect really crazy beers, serving the first Lambic drafts in Italy at Macché. "No one thought we would be able to sell these beers. Now if you put just one keg of Cantillon on tap, in two days, it's gone."

"Since that time, craft beer has become very popular," says Leonardo. "So many places started to open with the idea to use Italian craft beer instead of Belgian, German, or English beers. It was a very big explosion."

"The right people in the right place talking together," explains Marco Pion.

Entrance to Bir e Fud, just a few steps from Macché.

"Teo Musso, Agostino Arioli, Manuele Colonna, Leonardo Di Vincenzo in different ways are fundamental to the Italian movement," says Luca Giaccone. "Without the power, the credibility of Teo and Ago, maybe the movement wouldn't have exploded like it has. And without the extraordinary capacity of Manuele, maybe few bartenders would've followed."

In just two years, the world of Del Borgo has also changed. Profits shoot through the roof, and so does business. Del Borgo is ready to expand. Leonardo inaugurates a new brewery in 2009, not far from the existing brewery.

The new location has a store at the entrance, with a bar used for tastings. The walls are decorated with random outsider-style art. This is by far one of the largest breweries in Italy. To the side of the sophisticated brewhouse is a barrel room with various beers aging in different barrels. In the very back are the terra cotta fermenters used in the brewing of the Etruscan beer.

The more scientific side of Leonardo shows with this collaboration involving Sam Calagione from Dogfish Head, Teo Musso from

Terracotta vessels used to make Etrusca.

Baladin, Del Borgo, and molecular archaeologist Dr. Pat McGovern. Retracing ancient beverages discovered through chemical analysis of pottery shards found during digs, the four men try to recreate something that hasn't been made in more than 2,500 years. Each takes the same recipe drawn from the analysis of Etruscan pottery residue and brews the same beer.

Unsure of what the Etruscans might have fermented the beer in, each brewer chooses a different vessel. Calagione chooses copper, Teo chooses a wooden vessel, and Leonardo ferments his beer in terra cotta fermenters, which he has custom-made for the project. The results are all different. The terra cotta stands out as the most interesting because terra cotta is porous. The beer actually breathes in and out of the pores of the baked, earthen vessel, allowing some liquid out and some oxygen in. The throwback fermenters sitting in this modern brewery oozing beer ignite the imagination.

In another room is a very large rack with several hundred bottles resting inverted. Every day, each bottle is turned using the same method as champagne, collecting the yeast in the neck, from which it is eventually removed. This is the first edition of the Equilibrista. It's a blend of Duchessa and 50 percent Chianti grape juice, so it's Sangiovese grapes. After one year of fermentation, the champagne method is used to finish it.

155

"When we did this first one," explains Leonardo, "we only kept the grapes and the skin in for a few hours. The other times, we kept them in for two days. So, the beer gets a lot redder now with some astringency and tannin notes, much more complex."

"This is a demonstration that brewers don't do beer but they do wort," notes beer writer Luca Giaccone.

"Yeah, I really believe that," says Leonardo. "The real work is done by the yeast, not by us. Also, for example, here in Italy, we have a really big presence of different kinds of yeast, and I think that's important. Artisanal cheeses are made by different kinds of fermentation with different yeasts, not just one yeast. Normally, the brewing industry just uses one yeast, no variety. I think that's pretty cool, because here, you have this big variety, and so if you can keep this variety in your beer, you can have great complexity."

Under this philosophy, the old brewery becomes a laboratory for experimental brews and other innovative projects.

"The link between the wine world and the beer world—this is one very important point, speaking about fermentation," says Luca. "The richness of the yeast the wine culture can give to beer is something truly Italian and truly regional. If you brew in Lazio and you use a grape from Lazio, you put in the wort something that is unique. You won't find that anywhere else."

"Next April, we'll move all the stainless tanks out of the old brewery and just have wooden barrels," explains Leonardo. "We're going to add a koolschip, like they have at Cantillon, and we'll make only spontaneously fermented beers here at the original brewery. This will be our barrel house. We'll keep two stainless tanks here for making our fruit beer. We'll make our Prunus and Rubus—one is with raspberries and one is with cherries—and do them kind of like Lambics."

The new brewery is fitted with a bottling machine as well as a laboratory for quality control that extends to a weekly panel tasting that includes the staff and customers. Leonardo is leaving nothing to chance. From a lowly student hanging out with an American brewer and an up-and-coming chef, Leonardo Di Vincenzo (and Birra Del Borgo) has become synonymous with the future of Italian craft beer.

With Teo Musso and Sam Calagione in 2011, Leonardo launches La Birreria, a rooftop brewpub in the heart of Manhattan at the famous Italian food emporium Eataly. Once again, a great chef is a collaborator, Chef Mario Batali. Italian beer is now being featured to the Americans—Italian style.

In collaboration with Bonci, Luca Tosato, Paolo Bertani, and Teo, Leonardo opens NO.AU in 2012. In Piazza di Montevecchio near Piazza Navona in the heart of Rome, this unique Parisian bistro serves artisanal beer alongside wines to go with great food. NO.AU is an abbreviation that translates into Natural Organic Human Food in Italian.

It's been frequently mentioned in this book that Italians don't often get along, but Leonardo certainly eschews this cultural liability. Leonardo's success, unlike that of any other Italian brewer, expands quickly beyond his own borders. From brewer to publican to international figure, Leonardo has stepped up and pulled the Italian craft beer right up with him and will continue to do so.

"I've always admired Leonardo, who I own Bir e Fud with," reflects Manuele Colonna. "We'll collaborate on other things together. We essentially grew parallel together. It's been beautiful. The first Italian beer we put on was the ReAle. And then there was an explosion of all the other ones."

But the relationship between these two principal men hasn't stagnated. From a little misstep, an idea is finally going to come to fruition for Manuele. "The inspectors just noticed there's no window in the kitchen at Bir e Fud. Since this location was made into a restaurant as early as 1983, they haven't noticed. They just realized this, and they're forcing us to close it. Sincerely, I'm a little bit happy about it. The back area at Bir e Fud is now going to have thirty to forty taps. It'll just be pizza and apps because the kitchen has structural issues. This concept is something that's always on the edge because it's taxing with a lot of workers. The material is what it is, the rent is what it is. We want to rethink Bir e Fud a little bit, to relaunch it as this idea of many taps that Leo and I had been talking about. It was something that we revealed in conversation to Teo. Two weeks before the opening, I went to Open Baladin. When I saw it, I realized it wasn't just to open with fifty taps but also to cycle little cultural situations—doing like four or five taps that are Belgian, three or four from Franconia, some American, to give a cultural opportunity to the client. Not all Italian."

"Until Rome, no one was pushing for a beer pub," remembers Leonardo. "I think this was really important, the connection between Manuele, me, and the other publicans who started working on this. Everything was happening in Rome, and it was so important in the start-up of the beer market. About 10 percent of the market in Rome is craft beer, while in the rest of Italy, it's about 1 percent. It's incredible because in Rome now, you have a huge market.

"I think in Italy there are so many possible hot spots, places where the Italian craft-beer market can grow, big cities like Milan, Turin. The Italian craft-beer market has started to grow in other parts of Italy as well."

One place that even Leonardo couldn't have imagined would be in the Etruscan city of Palestrina. It's where Italy's food culture and craft beer finally meet.

Chapter 23
Coming into Its Own

By the time Marco Valente opens La Taberna in the tiny Etruscan fortress town of Palestrina forty minutes southeast of Rome, the Italian craft-beer movement has already taken off, but not in his area, not yet.

"Rome is a very important point of reference for artisanal beer. But in 2009, there was no artisanal beer in this area. I had never seen a Teku glass. It was a revelation."

Marco's been involved in pubs since he was young and has been plotting to open his own place for some time. He's worked for industrial breweries for years, and in 2001, Marco's job is to open bars for Guinness. Though he's been in the industry for many years, he doesn't hear of artisanal beer until 2007.

"That's when I knew I had to open this place."

After quitting his job, Marco spends a year working on his restaurant plan. "I wanted to open a restaurant, but I didn't want to abandon my knowledge of beer, so I merged them together. There was no particular location that inspired me. I was kind of looking for a personal revolution, to move towards a kitchen with high-end food. I designed it to be simple, yet modern."

Six months before opening La Taberna, Marco calls Leonardo Di Vincenzo of Birra Del Borgo. "I knew his beer, so I called him. My first tap was Leonardo's ReAle."

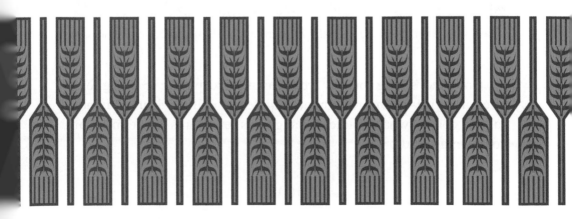

The entrance to La Taberna tucked away in the ancient Etruscan city of Palestrina.

Craft beer's long journey from gaining acceptance to being featured at a fine-dining restaurant is quite the cultural leap. It is not easy to convey what a radical change this represents in the mind of your average Italian.

Every detail of La Taberna is sharp and in its place. The barrel-vaulted ceiling extends back sixty feet to an ancient Etruscan wall. The wall, constructed of giant fitted stones, is part of the Temple of the Goddess Primigenia and dates back to 200 BCE. Houses used to be attached to the ancient wall but were razed during the bombings of World War II. Lit from below, the slightly yellowish wall, framed by the arched ceiling, glows like a warm sun. The classic yet modern simplicity is a reflection of Marco's modern concept.

Marco Valente serving guests with the ancient Etruscan wall in the background.

"My sister Irma and I opened La Taberna in 2009 with a focus on top-quality food with artisanal beer."

The food is exceptional, of course, offering local products on seasonal menus. The four menus feature gourmet dishes by Chef Massimiliano Tomasi that include pappardelle with duck in orange sauce and a sprinkle of cocoa, gnocchi, a chicken pie, goose prosciutto, and beef tenderloin stuffed with goat cheese and arugula. Only thirty-three years old, Marco is ahead of his age and time. No other place featuring Italian artisanal beer comes close to La Taberna's elegance and stature.

As the friendship between Leonardo and Marco deepens, Leonardo sees an opportunity. La Taberna can provide a place where people who don't want to enter Rome might find a way to experience the city's beer and food culture. La Taberna becomes *the* location to go to for Del Borgo beer outside of Rome.

"This place is the reference point for Leonardo's beer. We work with him on the experimental beer and work them into the pub. For us, personally, he gave a lot to this place. It wouldn't be what it is without his help. If you look on his website he refers to La Taberna as one of the most important places to go for Birra Del Borgo. And it's not like we've had a long relationship. We met each other just four years ago."

Leonardo visits often, and the two men collaborate on food pairings, showcasing new brewers as well as the established, older ones. Many of the pioneering brewers, judges, and writers frequent La Taberna. People such as Bruno Carilli from Toccalmatto, Luca Giaccone, Kuaska, and Teo Musso all baptize La Taberna.

As a publican, the one man who's given the most to Marco's launch is Manuele Colonna from Ma Che Siete Venuti A Fá in Rome. His battle to beat back the tidal wave of tied houses in Rome has set a precedent for any Italian who dreams of owning an independent bar.

"We already had the doors opened," remarks Marco. "Manuele is fundamental for us. We would've been nothing without him. This whole idea of changing up beer has just been born in Italy. Before, pubs poured the same beer for over ten years. There are obvious things people like here, but we change the rest. We do tastings every month and we feature an Italian brewer—Leonardo many times, but also Loverbeer, Montegioco, L'Olmaia, Rurale, Extraomnes, and so many more."

Before La Taberna, there were ten pubs in Palestrina, each doing the same thing, as all bars have been doing in Italy for what seems an eternity, but now, they all carry artisanal beer and handle it in their own way.

The brother and sister team, Irma and Marco Valente.

In the entire Italian beer world, nothing comes close to the classic elegance and sheer presence of La Taberna. It is an evolutionary concept, which finally brings Italian craft beer back around on itself. At La Taberna, it's not Baladin bottles being drunk in the kitchen, with the staff too ashamed to present the beer to their customers; rather, the beer is front and center and the wine is left in the kitchen to cook with.

Epilogue

Although we wish we could have included all the breweries in Italy, it just wasn't practical for one book. We weren't able to reach the Marche to interview Almond 22 and Opperbacco. And with time constraints, due to scheduling or the brewer's hours, we never had the chance to visit Troll, Brewfist, Croce di Malto, Ritorto, Pausa Café, Foglie D'Erba, San Paolo, Orso Verde, Extraomnes, or so many more. Regardless, the first ingredient in all Italian craft beer is passion. No matter which brewer, writer, publican, or restaurateur we spoke to, enthusiasm was always front and center. Along with passion, creativity is a hallmark of this scene.

At the grand-opening party for Birrificio Rurale's new location, the brewer, Lorenzo Guarino, allowed us a peek into an unexpected innovation on an old style. "It's a secret beer called the Italian Job. I haven't tasted it yet. It's going to be an Italian IPA where the finish is not coming from hops."

With the Italian Job, Lorenzo achieves the hop-like finish by utilizing a variety of bitter Calabrian orange peels. The bitterness sits on top of the tongue and lingers for a very long time. It's a different bitterness than the acidity you get from hops. We would call this an Italian Amaro IPA. It seems appropriate because the flavor is so reminiscent of the bitter orange liqueur, Amaro, which means bitter in Italian. It's very refreshing that a style so prevalent in the United

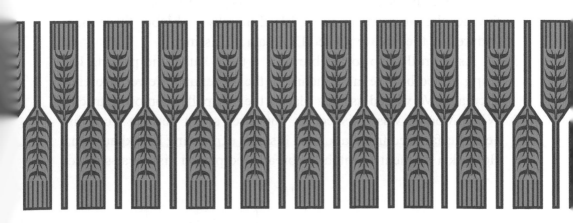

Lorenzo Guarino, head brewer at Birrificio Rurale, tasting the Italian Job for the first time.

States can be reimagined in a surprising way—it's definitely bitter but has only thirty-five IBUs.

Silvio Coppelli, founder of Birrificio Rurale, opened in 2009 with a lot of encouragement from Agostino Arioli of Birrificio Italiano. With Rurale's new location in Desio, an industrial area north of Milan, Silvio is considering the possibilities. While Rome is bustling with beer, the cities to the north, Turin and Milan, lag far behind, but with such big potential markets, these cities remain areas of opportunity.

"Just yesterday evening, I was at the Hilton hotel in Milan and the food and beverage manager told me he wanted to present a new image for their hotel," Silvio explains. "Because craft beer is a new trend here in Italy, they realized Rurale was a business they could work with and it's a way to differentiate themselves from the competition. For us, I think it could be a good opportunity."

Of course, creativity, innovation, and passion are all great ingredients for success, but they are nothing without the back-breaking work that implements them. There's no scarcity of an idle workforce in Italy, but with a restrictive system that often makes employees an unbearable financial burden, a lot of work has to be done by only a few people. No moment exemplified the physical labor these men endure like the day we visited L'Olmaia in Tuscany.

As we rolled up to the brewery, a truck sat in the parking lot being loaded by five men, including the owner and brewer, Moreno Ercolani. We waited as they placed the last pallets onto the truck. When Moreno was finished, we could see sweat pouring from his head, his face red from labor and his eyes expressing his exhaustion. He took a moment to catch his breath and placed his sweat-soaked

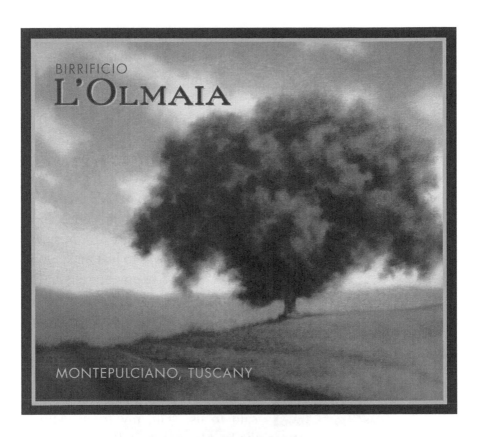

Moreno Ercolani, owner/brewer of L'Omaia.

face in his hands to rub away the fatigue. Then he began to tell us his story.

It wasn't long before his enthusiasm shined through.

His story was filled with tales of friendship and innovation. L'Olmaia's inception in 2004 was a leap in the dark, a gamble. Like many others before him, Moreno didn't have even the minimal idea of a business plan. The idea was to just make good beer. Moreno's hoppy style is at the forefront as the Italian tastes have expanded, and as new brewers are being born, they look to L'Olmaia for insights. Moreno is a testament to the brotherhood of these men.

As we prepared to leave, Moreno said to us, "Oh, my friend Mirko, who owns Bir & Fud Bottega, the best beer shop in Rome, now has a pub called Buskers Pub. It opened today."

Mirko Caretta characterizes a new type of brewer in Italy, the busker brewer, adapting to the environment in a very innovative way. Taking the name from the old buskers who hustled for money, playing music without a venue, gypsy brewing allows Mirko to brew without the overhead of a brewery.

"The first person I asked to brew with was Moreno from L'Olmaia. Once I made some beer with Moreno, other brewers offered, 'Come brew with us.' I said, 'No, I'll stay with Moreno,' and they said, 'What are we, assholes?' So I brewed at other places like Del Borgo, Extraomnes, BiDu, and Opperbacco starting in 2010. I never ended up with my own brewery because this was just so much easier."

Throughout our travels, one of the things that reminded us of the infancy of the overall Italian craft-beer market was how small some of these breweries are. Even the big guys are small compared to

American standards of today. A brewery like Russian River in California supplies only a handful of markets in the United States, yet it brews more beer than Teo Musso at Baladin. Russian River is tiny, but it would be a giant in Italy.

Authors, Paul Vismara (left) and Bryan Jansing (center) at Mirko Caretta's (right) Buskers Pub on their second day of business.

"If you think of Valter Loverier at Loverbeer or Riccardo at Montegioco, they are really small," observed Bruno Carilli from Toccalmatto. "They are producing some of the best beer in Italy, or Europe, for that matter. Valter is producing about 200 hectoliters (160 barrels) a year. It's more like a home brewer."

"Vinnie Cilurzo from Russian River is a brewer that, in my opinion, is parallel to Valter," said Teo Musso. "According to me, in Italy, we've gone down a road where the only producer from the new generation that's interesting is Valter."

"My mission was to use recipes from the Flemish area," said Valter, "and join it with the wine-making culture of Piedmont. For this reason, we use fruit and grapes like Barbera grapes, Nebbiolo, and

Dulcetto. I'm sure in ancient times, other people thought to put grapes in beer, but now it seems like an original idea to use grapes post-fermentation."

Valter Loverier in front of one of his wooden barrel vats.

Using local ingredients has become more common in the United States, but Italians have always thought that way. Since opening Loverbeer in 2009, Valter has had the idea to be faithful to the old Belgian methods, but being Italian, he reimagines the traditional Belgian Kriek using local Ramassin del Saluzzese plums in his Beer Brugna.

He has the only Italian brewery entirely devoted to barrel-aged, sour beer. This is a rarity, not only in Italy, but in the world. Of course, Valter's path had already been carved at the dawn of the Italian craft movement by the MIA brewer Renzo Losi from Panil.

In February 2013, like a phoenix rising from the ashes, Renzo Losi reinvents himself as Birrificio Black Barrel. Renzo has decided to become a gypsy brewer and blender, in the tradition of the great Belgian beer blenders. Located in the heart of Turin, Black Barrel is a small, narrow beer shop with bottles lining shelves on either wall. Renzo's cantina is downstairs, where he ages his beer in a growing collection of barrels.

"The beer is being reborn from the barrel, barrels that had wine in them and some that were used for grappa," explains Renzo. "Barrels are part of our culture, they're all around us. It's going to take some time before the cantina expresses its yeast. The barrels have to slowly, slowly create their story—two or three years. It's nothing that can happen quickly."

All the foundational breweries are now seventeen years old and stand on solid ground. They are growing, if they choose to, despite the obstacles. There's no going back. We're happy to say you'll never have to travel to Italy and drink bad beer again. Even better, more and more Italian craft-beer is finding its way around the world. The new breweries are brewing with a ready audience, a far cry from the pioneers' early experiences.

With the excitement that runs through this fledgling beer community, there's no telling what they can do or will do. We can't wait to find out.

CPSIA information can be obtained at www.ICGtesting.com
Printed in the USA
LVOW01s0629190314

378025LV00003B/9/P